The First Verb

The First Verb

Cultivating Christian Creativity

Colleen Warren

CASCADE *Books* • Eugene, Oregon

THE FIRST VERB
Cultivating Christian Creativity

Copyright © 2024 Colleen Warren. All rights reserved. Except for brief quotations in critical publications or reviews, no part of this book may be reproduced in any manner without prior written permission from the publisher. Write: Permissions, Wipf and Stock Publishers, 199 W. 8th Ave., Suite 3, Eugene, OR 97401.

Cascade Books
An Imprint of Wipf and Stock Publishers
199 W. 8th Ave., Suite 3
Eugene, OR 97401

www.wipfandstock.com

PAPERBACK ISBN: 978-1-6667-8526-5
HARDCOVER ISBN: 978-1-6667-8527-2
EBOOK ISBN: 978-1-6667-8528-9

Cataloguing-in-Publication data:

Names: Warren, Colleen, 1959–, author.

Title: The first verb : cultivating Christian creativity / Colleen Warren.

Description: Eugene, OR: Cascade Books, 2024. | Includes bibliographical references.

Identifiers: ISBN 978-1-6667-8526-5 (paperback). | ISBN 978-1-6667-8527-2 (hardcover). | ISBN 978-1-6667-8528-9 (ebook).

Subjects: LSCH: Creativity—Religious aspects—Christianity. | Christian life. | Creation (Literary, artistic, etc.).

Classification: BT709.5 W38 2024 (print). | BT709.5 (epub).

VERSION NUMBER 02/07/24

All Scripture quotations, unless otherwise indicated, are taken from the Holy Bible, New International Version®, NIV®. Copyright ©1973, 1978, 1984, 2011 by Biblica, Inc.™ Used by permission of Zondervan. All rights reserved worldwide. www.zondervan.com

In 2010, I published my first book, a realization of a life-long dream that so thrilled and awed me that I would have been content, at the time, for it to be my last and only book. But publication brought with it a growing desire to continue writing; I knew then that working with words—their sounds in my mouth, the whisper of a pen spilling them out onto a blank page, the magic of scribbled outlines being transformed from bare bones into fully fleshed concepts—was something I wanted to do, maybe even *had* to do, the rest of my life.

Writing has been a path I've followed since sixth grade, when my teacher Mrs. Curl began tacking my paragraphs to the bulletin board, igniting my ambitions to be a Semi-Famous Small-Town Author. From there, majoring in English in college, working as a high school English teacher, returning to college to get an MA and a PhD in American literature, and traveling on a trail as a college professor have been milestones in my journey. Along the way, many acquaintances, colleagues, fellow students, and friends have shared different moments of that trip with me. But the journey has taken me away from most of them to new places, has given me new roles, has altered even the type of traveler I am. There are few constants in a journey such as this, but this book is dedicated to a person who has been such a constant—my husband Jim.

Because he's traveled with me, the journey has changed him too. When we launched out, I don't think either of us had any idea how much the trip would affect us, either individually or as a couple. There are times when my writing demands a lot of my time, a solitary concentration that takes time away from our relationship. But over the years, I've seen him adapt to accommodate my desire to write, not only because he loves me but because he himself sees the worth in what I am writing and shares my commitment to the purpose of my writing, a purpose that has become more sharply focused with every book I write: to point out to readers paths that will lead them closer to God.

So thank you, Jim, for giving me space, for being a sounding board, for seeing beyond the daily sacrifices to the eternal impact both of us value above all else. Though we've stumbled some over the years and tripped a bit, I'm grateful for the trails writing has allowed me to explore, and happy that you've been beside me for most of the journey, both of us walking in the same direction.

When I consider your heavens,
the work of your fingers,
the moon and the stars,
which you have set in place,
what is mankind that you are mindful of them,
human beings that you care for them?

—Psalm 8:3–4

The aim of any art is to represent not the outward appearance,
but the inward significance.

—Aristotle

Art evokes the mystery without which
the world would not exist.

—René Magritte

Creativity is not a mood. Creativity is not a gift.
It's the very nature of God inside of you.

—Dan McCollum

Contents

Acknowledgments | ix

1 God's Creativity | 1
2 Emulating God: The Command to Create | 26
3 Committing to Creativity and Maintaining an Artistic Mindset | 37
4 The Benefits of Creativity | 55
5 A Theology of Creativity | 66
6 Establishing a Practice and Place | 97
7 Practices that Increase Creativity | 107
8 Art the Father Loves | 124

Bibliography | 129

Acknowledgments

THOUGH MY ACTUAL WRITING is, for me, a solitary activity, there were many people who helped shape this book towards publication. At the personal, everyday level, my husband, Jim, gave me good suggestions that helped me frame the first chapter, and throughout the process, gave me the time and solitude I needed to draft and revise the manuscript; my daughter Faith added encouragement through her love for me and with her frequent proclamations of My General Worth and Value.

At a more technical level, I want to thank Matthew Wimer, managing editor at Wipf and Stock, for patiently waiting for my signed contract and promptly answering the many questions I bombarded him with in the first weeks of our interaction. I would also like to thank Caleb Shupe, copyeditor and format checker at Wipf and Stock, for his painstaking and time-consuming attention to my manuscript; he is largely responsible for the professional appearance of the final manuscript and the accuracy of my citations. My colleague in the English department, Dan Bowman, and my former colleague and continued friend, Jim Spiegel, graciously agreed to thoughtfully and thoroughly read my manuscript and write a blurb for the back cover, a service they contributed for my last book as well. I am also greatly honored that Michael Card, whose work I admire and to whom I refer extensively in this book, was willing to recommend it to others.

And a shout out to the women in my different Bible study groups at Upland Community Church, who possibly don't even know the extent to which they encouraged me in my creativity. One group's spirited participation in a

ACKNOWLEDGMENTS

study of my last book and another group's interest in my altered books and other art projects, their provision for me as I recovered from a severed rotator cuff, and their prayers as I worked through my drafts and sent proposals to publishers were more meaningful than I can express.

My deepest gratitude, however, and the greatest indebtedness I have, is to God, whose bountiful beauty, extravagant excess, deep design, and jubilant joy make all human creativity possible.

1

God's Creativity

THE FIRST VERB, THE verb that launched the world into existence and set into motion existence itself, was *created*. "In the beginning, God *created* the heavens and the earth." *Create*. To start with nothing, and out of that nothing to make something, and more than something—*all* things, a whirling universe of perfect design, a vast cosmological collection of all things beautiful, symmetrical, and ordered. God *created*. Though God, in his power, could have silently willed the world into being, he chose to speak, calling forth each element with his Word. God *said*. Sometimes he only gazed in satisfaction at the world unfurling at his feet. God *saw*. At other points he more actively intervened, *separating* the light from the darkness or the waters from the sky, *gathering* the waters into seas and forming dry ground.

Thirty creation verbs after the first *created*, humanity came into existence. "Then God said, 'Let us make mankind in our image, in our likeness'" (Gen 1:26 NIV).[1] For the first time in the written record, God reveals himself as a triune being, a harmonious, multifaceted creator, referring to himself with the pronouns *us* and *our*, making man in the image of the Trinity, describing his creation as both an artistic endeavor, a sculpture he "formed from the dust of the ground" as well as a creature to whom he gave spiritual birth: "and [he] breathed into his nostrils the breath of life, and the man became a living being" (2:7). Adam was perfect, but incomplete—an unsung song, a painting not yet displayed, a dance as

---

1. Throughout, unless otherwise noted, scriptural references will be taken from the New International Version.

yet unperformed. How long a span of time do the six verses represent that describe Adam existing alone? How long did it take for Adam to feel the ache of his own incompleteness?

Waking one morning, he felt for the first time a sense of something changed. Created as distinct and unique, yet also made in a manner that reflected in small measure the oneness of God's Trinitarian identity, woman was made from a part of man, the significance of which was not lost on Adam, for his first words regarding her express the bond that he felt between them. "'This is now bone of my bone and flesh of my flesh'" (2:23), the heart of the marriage and sexual covenant. Just as God had given names to confirm the individuality and importance of each part of creation, so did Adam name Eve, choosing a name, appropriately, that was a derivation of his own: *woman*, which means "from man."

Creation. The details of this event, initiated in a time before time existed, would be lost to us were it not for the Word, who preexisted creation itself. Again, God gave of himself and blessed mankind with the gift of language; ultimately the author of Genesis, emulating God's own method of creation, used words to re-create creation, and through his account we too can see and say that it was good.

Creativity is the first and fundamental attribute of God, his ability to begin with nothing and produce something, an *ex nihilo* act which we cannot comprehend or duplicate, but which we accept in fumbling awe because all the alternate explanations—random chance, the Big Bang—are even more incredible to believe and utterly fail to account for the complexity and perfection that creation contains. Jeremiah declares the truth that "God made the earth by his wisdom and stretched out the heavens by his understanding" (Jer 10:12). Implicit in his assertion is that his own power, wisdom, and understanding are too limited to wrap his mind around the magnitude of such a God and such an act, and we too must acknowledge our inadequacy to comprehend. Though our dearth of understanding should establish in us a profound humility, we reveal our fundamental arrogance in assuming the world was made for our pleasure. Yet the creation of the entire natural world preceded human existence, since we were the last element of God's creative plan, a fact that suggests that God initiated creation at first for his own delight, a supposition that Col 1:16 confirms when it claims that all things were created "through him and *for* him." Thus, when I picture the process of creation, I imagine God as an artist, absorbed in his work, adding one element at a time to his art, giving individual attention to each shape and color he added to the huge expanse of his dark, empty canvas. He wasted no space—there were no false starts, no blots or errors, no slip of his brush or poor sketches. The elements he created could be nothing other than good, because the Creator himself is only good. Each day he stood before his easel and added something that made the good better, layers of complexity and design and beauty so grand that they unfurled into limitless space, expanding, becoming animate, self-perpetuating.

I believe that God took joy in his creation and that the process he chose extended his pleasure. God could have created all that exists instantaneously and simultaneously, with just a thought, but he did not. Instead, he lingered over every element of nature, creating it in stages, bit by bit, to prolong his delight. God reveled in the creative process, allowing full range to his imagination, spreading beauty with broad brushstrokes, creating the very concept of beauty as he formed his art: symmetry, order, design, balance, function, complementary colors, form, cohesion—all the elements that constitute what we consider beautiful are displayed in the created universe, and our own definition of beauty originates in God's own nature. The beauty he created emanated from his own beauty; his art was an expression of himself. Nor were the elements of creation mere materials, like paint or paper or musical notes—they were part of him, and he loved and valued each part so much so that he gave each an identity, a name: Day. Night. Sky. Land. Seas.

After the dazzling days of creation were completed, however, and humanity had been added as a culminating lagniappe of his artistry, in an astounding demonstration of his love for mankind and the extent to which he desired for them to share in his creative energy and joy, God established Adam and Eve as not only caretakers but cocreators alongside him, allowing them to assist him in naming the elements of his creation, trusting them to maintain and even reshape Eden through the "dominion" he granted them, and to enlarge and expand its beauty through their reproductive ability.

Centuries later, God reasserted his creative power and again invited humanity to create alongside him when God decided to construct a house for his dwelling, a tangible tabernacle to give substance to his unwavering yet invisible presence among the Israelites. As Jordan Raynor points out, the tabernacle paralleled God's creation of the universe, in that it existed as its own world, with every element pointing to God and every element designed by God himself, a fact that confirms God's continued delight in his own creativity,[2] evident in the extraordinarily detailed specifications for the design of the tabernacle recorded in Exod 25–27, 35–40 and repeated in part in Num 1, 3–7, and 9–10. God alone designed every minute feature of his "home" and dictated his plans to Moses at the same time that he imparted the Ten Commandments and the voluminous laws the Israelites were to follow, indicating the similar importance of his creative orders and explaining why it took Moses a month and a half to return from Sinai! God's designs for the tabernacle are so exact in their specifications that they make for some of the most tedious reading in the Bible, outdone only by the endless genealogies of unpronounceable names. However, such detail also asserts God's investment in creativity and art. As architect, God specified its dimensions, design, and floor plan and designed it as a portable building, constructed as an elaborate system of poles, hanging tapestries and animal skins, with a roof of skins. As contractor, he calculated the number and lengths of the poles, the optimal spacing of the poles and rings which supported the walls, and the number of skins necessary to enclose the roof. As craftsman and carpenter, he designed all the furnishings, including the tables, chairs, basins, candle stands, altars, incense holders—even the bowls, cups, and utensils used for the sacrifices. As interior decorator, he determined the color of the thread and the designs to be woven into the tapestries that divided the rooms and ordered the arrangements of the furniture. God dictated every detail of the tabernacle's construction to Moses, information that Moses faithfully recorded in all its exactness.

Though God himself determined the design and construction of the tabernacle, planning it not only as a showcase of beauty but a marvel of functionality and practicality, he didn't—though he could have—actually construct the building with his own hands, as he did at the creation of the world. Instead, he chose to collaborate with a huge company of craftsmen, a decision which confirms that he wants humans to actively express their own creativity and skills in service to him.

That God wanted the tabernacle to be a celebration of communal creativity is obvious by the wide variety of artists who contributed to the effort. First and foremost, he chose a man called Bezalel to be the general contractor, supervising the work and serving as master craftsman, along with his aide, Oholiab. Importantly, Bezalel is the first person in the Bible to be identified as filled with the Spirit,[3] and it is God's Spirit who endows

---

2. Raynor, "New Series," para. 5.
3. Liesch and Finley, "Biblical Concept," 43.

Bezalel with the three traits that are necessary to the creativity that emulates God's own: wisdom, understanding, and knowledge. These qualities, as Prov 3:19–20 confirms, were the same elements that guided God's own creation of the world: "By wisdom the Lord laid the earth's foundations, by understanding he set the heavens in place; by his knowledge the deeps were divided and the clouds let drop the dew." Using Prov 24:3–4, a passage that valorizes the same three traits and which uses a metaphor that corresponds well to the construction of the tabernacle, Dan McCollam associates wisdom with ingenuity ("by wisdom a house is built"), understanding with sustainability ("and through understanding it is established"), and knowledge with profitability ("through knowledge its rooms are filled with rare and beautiful treasures").[4] These three elements could be equally aligned in these verses with imagination, structural integrity, and aesthetic awareness.

Over and over in Scripture, these same three qualities are identified as traits possessed by people who were especially gifted by God in intelligence and creativity, including Solomon (1 Kgs 4:29), Shadrach, Meshach, and Abednego (Dan 1:17), Daniel (Dan 2:21–23), and Jesus himself (Isa 11:2).[5] Perhaps most importantly, these are also the qualities that enable an intimate relationship with God, according to Prov 9:10—"The fear of the Lord is the beginning of wisdom, and knowledge of the Holy One is understanding." What a wonderful confluence of benefit is suggested in valuing and cultivating these traits in ourselves: both increased creativity and an enriched relationship with the God of creation! As believers in Christ, we have access to, incredibly, "the mind of Christ" (Col 2:2–3) and our bodies become "temples of the Holy Spirit" (1 Cor 6:19), capabilities that more than adequately qualify us to emulate God's creativity.

Because the indwelling of the Holy Spirit in Bezalel is explicitly noted to be the origin of Bezalel's creativity and the source of his wisdom, understanding, and knowledge, we can be assured that the Holy Spirit enables, directs, and values all creativity, not just explicitly spiritual abilities and gifts. Matt Tommey goes even further in noting Bezalel's qualifications for the creative work he led by noting the etymologies of the names associated with Bezalel and his family history. Tommey points out that *Bezalel* means "in the shadow or protection of God" and that his father's name,

---

4. McCollam, *All about Releasing Creativity*, Day 1.
5. McCollam, *All about Releasing Creativity*, Day 1.

Uri, characterizes him as "the fiery one, light, prophetic revelation."[6] His grandfather's name, *Hur,* adds the quality of whiteness or purity, and Bezalel's tribal association, *Judah,* indicates that Bezalel will do his work for the *praise* of God. Tommey uses these etymologies to conclude that Bezalel, and, by extension, all who share in God's creativity, are people protected and called by God to create with purity and praise, using our art as a prophetic light that will guide others to Christ.[7]

Not only was Bezalel especially gifted to orchestrate the creative work on the tabernacle, but he and his coworker Oholiab were surrounded by a huge contingent of gifted Israelites representing nearly every area of craftsmanship and artistry imaginable, working at God's invitation: "All who are skilled among you are to come and make everything the Lord has commanded" (Exod 35:10). Both men and women participated. Among them were builders, blacksmiths, silversmiths, goldsmiths, furniture makers, tanners, hunters, tailors, embroiderers, dyers, jewelers, gardeners, perfumers, bakers, and candle makers. In addition to their participation in the actual construction of the tabernacle, the people also provided the materials for the construction, a detail that suggests that the *support* of the arts is another form of artistic contribution just as valid as the process of making art.

> Everyone who is willing is to bring to the Lord an offering of gold, silver and bronze; blue, purple and scarlet yarn and fine linen; goat hair; ram skins dyed red and another type of durable leather; acacia wood; olive oil for the light; spices for the anointing oil and for the fragrant incense; and onyx stones and other gems to be mounted on the ephod and breast piece. (Exod 35:5–9)

Though God *invited* all the Israelites to participate in some aspect of the temple construction, he did not *require* it; God wanted their involvement to be voluntary and joyful, entered into with a willing spirit, a mindset that is evoked five times in Exod 35 alone (Exod 35:5, 21, 22, 26, 29); the wording of 35:21 is representative: "And everyone who was willing and whose heart moved them." This joyful, uncoerced creativity resulted in at least two positive outcomes: first, the people gave an excess of contributions (Exod 36:5–7), evidence of the nearly universal emotional and spiritual investment of the people in being a part of this venture. Secondly, God was pleased with the Israelites' submission to his

6. Tommey, *Unlocking the Heart,* Day 1.
7. Tommey, *Unlocking the Heart,* Day 1.

design, their obedience in following exactly the plans he had laid out, and the individual creative expertise each artist brought to the task. He confirmed his pleasure by inhabiting the home they had constructed, filling it with his shekinah glory, his ultimate, final contribution to the tabernacle, perfecting their art (Exod 40:34–38). Because the purpose of their creativity was to honor God, God increased the significance of their art; it became more than a tent—it became their guidance through the cloud that hovered over the tabernacle by day and the fire-filled cloud by night, a constant reminder of God's presence among them.

The contexts and conditions so strongly emphasized in the construction of the tabernacle are just as applicable to our creative lives today. God endows all of us with creative potential, though our creativity varies greatly in expression and in measure for each individual. Though he has gifted us all, the exercise of our creativity remains our personal decision. And, as the example of the tabernacle makes clear, all forms of creativity are best used in service and gratitude to God, the source and sustainer of our creativity. When this is our purpose, God will bless our efforts and increase the import and effects of our art, making it more than it could ever be through our efforts alone.

As carefully designed, functional, and beautiful as the tabernacle was, and all the more beautiful because of the collaborative creativity that constructed it, it could not, of course, contain the God of the universe. Even the later grandiose temple that Solomon erected as a permanent "home" for God, as he himself admitted, was inadequate to house the majesty of God: in his prayer of dedication, Solomon declared, "But will God really dwell on earth? The heavens, even the highest heaven, cannot contain you. How much less this temple I have built!" (1 Kgs 8:27)

Still, both structures were emblematic of God's desire to establish his presence among his people. Given this, the temple, and perhaps to an even greater degree the tabernacle, since it was of God's design, prefigure God's most amazing creative act—the incarnation. In the incarnation, God fashioned *himself* into a work of art that literalized his desire to dwell among us: the temple was now God himself made flesh. God was deliberate and intentional in fashioning the human form he would take. Given my focus here, I think it especially significant that God chose to give himself the profession of a carpenter, a craftsman-creative position he practiced for 85 percent of his life.[8] Beyond this, he chose a form which was not an

---

8. Raynor, "New Series," para. 5.

ultimate manifestation of beauty (Isa 53:2) but a form consummately human to express God's supreme valuation of humanity, a form malleable to service, despite the divinity it housed; a form, seemingly ordinary, yet housing the extraordinary, and most significantly, a form capable of being destroyed—as all art is—yet uniquely capable of self-renewal, autonomous regeneration—a capacity human art lacks. And miraculously, far beyond this, the incarnation, unlike our human creations that can only aspire to provoke thought and convey meaning, was the embodiment of meaning and truth itself. Language as art, in Christ, was the Living Word—not existing as static marks on dead paper but actively marking souls for eternal life. "Through the Incarnation, art as sacrifice and art as service become art as sacrament. This sacramental view of nature and human nature converts every natural object and every positive act into a testament to God's grace. . . . If art is sacrifice and service, then . . . [the Incarnation] is God's consummate work of art."[9]

All of God's creative products—the world, Eden, the tabernacle, the incarnation—confirm the superlative nature of God's creativity; that is, *adequate* is not a word we can use to describe God's creativity. God's art is not merely attractive or pleasing; it is bountifully beautiful. Nor can it be characterized as merely sufficient, for God's creativity encompasses far more range and grandeur than is "necessary"—he delights in extravagant excess. Likewise, God does not casually plan the general arrangement of his creations—he deeply designs every infinitesimal element. And, when God engages in creative activity, it is not for him just an enjoyable diversion; he exhibits an intensity of pleasure in creativity, a jubilant joy that he evidences in his playful, even quirky, creative output.

Even a casual, cursory glance at nature confirms that the world contains bountiful beauty. Beauty is intrinsic to who God is, and the world dazzles us with multiple displays of his love of the aesthetic. God scatters fragments of his beauty, like sown seeds, over all creation. Though beauty sometimes aligns with function, at other times it is often wonderfully gratuitous, and if God had not created us with an innate *need* for beauty, we could argue that aesthetics were superfluous—unnecessary frills and adornment. However, when God created beauty, he also created humans to have a craving for beauty and an appreciation for it. As Eric Carlson notes, our attraction to beauty is not just superficial, but a crucial way in which we understand the world around us—it aids in establishing relationships

---

9. Lockerbie, *Timeless Moment*, 29, 28.

with each other and with our environment and even affects such simple and relatively insignificant things as how we respond to our food.[10] Studies show that we think better and are less depressed when we surround ourselves with beautiful spaces. Cody Delistraty, in "A Neurological Defense of Aestheticism: Why Our Brains Crave Beauty," confirms this function of beauty, arguing that humans need beauty to sustain their mental health, commenting that exposure to beauty reduces stress, increases energy, and even establishes trust in others.[11]

Our attraction to and our desire for beauty originates in our *imago dei* identities. God instilled within each of us his own passion for the beautiful and provided infinite ways to satisfy that desire. From the very beginning, for example, there is evidence that God created Eden primarily as a showcase for beauty, an integral feature of its design, more than as simply a practical living space for Adam and Eve.[12] The first details of its description in Gen 2:9 suggest this. The biblical narrative mentions the aesthetics of its trees before it notes their functionality, commenting that they "were pleasing to the eye and good for food." Symmetry and design are evident in the centrality of the Tree of Life and the Tree of the Knowledge of Good and Evil and in the river that perfectly bisects the garden. The garden of Eden: an ideal climate, a profusion of birds and beasts and flowers and fruit, clear skies lit by God's radiance, soft breezes that stirred with Spirit—a paradisiacal place designed to fulfill the human need for beauty that God ingrained within each of us.

God's emphasis on beauty in creation is just as evident today. Refraction of light could have been a colorless affair, but instead he gave us rainbows and prisms, a gorgeous spectrum of colors even on dreary, gray, rain-drenched days. Snowflakes could have been shapeless blobs of ice, but instead each is a unique and delicate miracle of symmetry and radiating design, pure and sparkling white. All birds could have been voiceless or—worse—could have had a crow's call, undifferentiated from each other. Yet he chose to give each bird its own song and quality of sound, some with only a single aubade to offer, and some, like the mockingbird, able to replicate dozens of calls. Flowers could have been excised from creation, their function of pollination met by any drab plant, but God chose to "cast [them] broadside from a

---

10. Carlson, "Why Beauty Is Important."
11. Delistraty, "Neurological Defense," para. 6.
12. Terry and Lister, *Images and Idols*, 33.

generous hand"[13] in a stunning variety of sizes, colors, and shapes, from the vivid, waxy red cups of tulips to the pale, delicately veined spring beauties, one of the first woodland flowers to announce spring. Beyond their physical beauty, flowers also offer scents that delight us—the thick sweetness of honeysuckle, the fresh scent of lilacs, the woodsy sweetness of the narcissus. How ordinary our days would be, how spiritless our mornings and how anticlimactic our evenings without the light shows of sunrises and sunsets! To replace a pre-creation darkness and void with glowing, melting ribbons of orange, violet, and yellow, ribbons that change hues and brightness and swirl into different layers as the rising sun pulses through them—this is a design of beauty only God could have conceived. And, to add blessing upon blessing, he closes each day with an equally stunning show, as if to assure us that the heaving ball of fire will not sizzle and extinguish in the ocean into which it sinks or be buried in the dark horizon that swallows it. The world is so "charged with the grandeur of God," as Gerard Manley Hopkins puts it,[14] that it is impossible to enumerate all the examples. Beauty is a preeminent quality of God's creative genius.

And this profligate abandon is yet another quality of God's creativity. He never creates minimally, with tight-fisted economy or in carefully measured amounts. His creativity is always an extravagant excess, a mind-blowing grandness, the primary purpose of which, I am convinced, is to remind us, over and over, that his ways are higher than ours, that we cannot even begin to conceive of his bigness, his glory. Consider trees, seemingly a quite ordinary and certainly a common element of creation. Yet how could an artist paint even one tree, even in a lifetime, with all its intricacy and detail? To reproduce every furrow and crease in the bark, to draw every split of a branch, each branch into its boughs, limbs dividing into twigs and sprigs would be painstaking work. Yet the most difficult task of all would be to capture in paint every individual leaf, which scientists estimate number in the hundreds of thousands for each tree and as much as a million on a fully grown oak. Could the artist duplicate each hue of green, each distinct shape, notched, bitten, and frayed?

Yet as intricate as trees are, they pale in their grandness when juxtaposed against the seas' scope. Water covers 71 percent of the planet.[15] It varies in depth from an inch at the shore, sliding upon the sand, to

---

13. Dillard, *Pilgrim*, 15.
14. Hopkins, "God's Grandeur," 1.1.
15. Webb, "Overview of the Oceans," para. 1.

36,200 feet (almost seven miles!) in the Challenger Deep, located in the western Pacific Ocean.[16] This is only an estimate, since humans are incapable, even when encased in machines, of fully plumbing the depths. In addition, the sheer surface area of the oceans makes it impossible to fully explore. The total area of the world's oceans is over 139 million square miles, and given its average depth of 12,500 feet, its volume is about 1.37 billion cubic kilometers.[17]

Between 226,000[18] and 240,000[19] species of sea life have been discovered and classified, yet that mind boggling number represents only 9 *percent* of the sea life present in the oceans. In other words, about 91 percent of all sea life is still undiscovered, because we have explored less than 20 percent of the ocean.[20] Every year, we discover an average of 2,000 new species; about 150 of that 2,000 are fish. If we retain our present rate of discovery, it would take over thirty years just to discover the number of *fish* species scientists believe exist in the oceans.[21] Even with discovery rates exponentially growing, and with more discoveries in the last twenty years than in most of the time preceding that, still we have 80 percent of the oceans yet to explore and have 91 percent of the sea life within them yet to discover and catalog. Just considering fish alone, scientists estimate that there are 3.5 quadrillion in the seas.[22] This number is literally unfathomable. For example, even if you could count one fish per second, it would take 31,685 years to count only one trillion of them. To count one quadrillion of the over three quadrillion that are in the oceans would take over 31 million years. If human beings have existed on the earth for six thousand years, and even with our current knowledge and resources have explored and discovered only a tiny fraction of what God has created in a region of the earth that surrounds us on every side, I have to conclude that God created such excess only to make the rather obvious point that we can't possibly come close to knowing the extent of his creative range.

16. Webb, "Overview of the Oceans," para. 3.
17. Webb, "Overview of the Oceans," para. 3.
18. United Nations Educational, Scientific and Cultural Organization, "Ocean Life," para. 1.
19. Flanders Marine Institute, "Number of Marine Species," para. 1.
20. National Oceanic and Atmospheric Administration, "How Many Species," para. 2.
21. United Nations Educational, Scientific and Cultural Organization, "Ocean Life," paras. 3–4.
22. Chepkemoi, "How Many Fish," para. 1.

As overwhelming as these examples are, nothing is greater evidence of God's extravagant excess than the cosmos. What I have been describing are things contained within our planet; the Earth is the world to us, the sum of everything that exists. Even what the Earth, a mere spot in a small galaxy, contains, as I have shown, is beyond our comprehension. Yet if compared to the largest planet in our galaxy, Earth shrinks in significance. Earth is 13,000 kilometers in diameter, or 8077.826 miles, yet Jupiter is 140,000 kilometers in diameter, over ten times bigger.[23] If we follow this expansion out into space, the diameter of the sun, which is only a *dwarf* star, is 1,400,000 kilometers, ten times bigger than Jupiter, yet the sun is only a fraction of the size of Elnath, a giant star whose diameter is 5,800,000 kilometers.[24] *Aludra*, a supergiant star, is 80,000,000 kilometers,[25] but V4 *Cannis Majoris*, a hypergiant star, is more than double that at two billion kilometers.[26] This star, however, is hugely overshadowed in size by one of the millions of supermassive black holes that exists, which is 240 trillion kilometers.[27] At this point, though we humans now have technology that enables us to observe much farther into the known universe, we have run out of numbers large enough to express the size of some of the elements this distant from us. Thus, scientists started measuring size in terms of light-years. A single light-year represents almost 9.5 trillion kilometers,[28] and a nebula appropriately called "Eye of God" is 2.6 light-years in diameter, a number inconceivable to us,[29] yet the Milky Way galaxy, the galaxy the Earth exists within, makes Eye of God seem small, for it is 100,000,000 light-years in diameter.[30] Yet the Milky Way is only one of 100–200 *billion* galaxies that scientists believe to be in the universe. Within the Milky Way alone, scientists estimate that there are over one hundred billion stars, and in the entire universe, one scientist estimated that there are over 1 septillion stars (that's 1 with 24 zeros after it!); as outrageously large as this number seems, the scientist claimed that even this largesse was probably a huge underestimate.[31] Our instruments have "seen" up to 150

---

23. Estudio Arkano, "Your Mind Will Collapse," 1:04.
24. Estudio Arkano, "Your Mind Will Collapse," 1:31.
25. Estudio Arkano, "Your Mind Will Collapse," 1:51.
26. Estudio Arkano, "Your Mind Will Collapse," 2:12.
27. Estudio Arkano, "Your Mind Will Collapse," 2:46.
28. Estudio Arkano, "Your Mind Will Collapse," 3:06.
29. Estudio Arkano, "Your Mind Will Collapse," 3:07.
30. Estudio Arkano, "Your Mind Will Collapse," 3:50.
31. Harvey, "How Many Stars," para. 17.

GOD'S CREATIVITY

billion light-years from the earth, what scientists refer to as the "Observable Universe," and from that point to 250 million light-years away, they regard as empty space,[32] calling that expanse the Great Nothing, which of course is a huge misnomer. Lying on our backs on the grass-covered, familiar solidity of planet Earth, we with our naked eyes can see literally countless stars; to think that these represent only a miniscule number of all the stars, black holes, nebulas, and galaxies out there gives us a tiny inkling of how greatly we underestimate the bigness of God and the extent of his creativity.

With such profusion, it would be reasonable to expect that much of creation would exist randomly, with little regulation or order. After all, since such an excess exists, what would it matter if a certain percentage spun off uncontrolled or self-destructed? Yet this does not seem to be the case; rather, perfect precision and deep design seem to characterize all of God's creation, and most of us are not aware or do not acknowledge the extent to which this is true, even in the smallest, most common elements of nature. Most of us, for example, have often observed or at least have heard the sound of a woodpecker drilling into a tree, but few of us are aware of the marvel of design that allows this. Big, brawny NFL players are susceptible to concussions when equally big, brawny NFL players hit them, despite their helmeted protection. For example, every year from 2012 to 2019, 242 NFL players, on average, suffered concussions.[33] Overall, about one third of NFL players have long-term brain damage as a result.[34] A g-force of only sixty to one hundred can result in concussions, yet woodpeckers, although they seem to have fragile little heads and wear no helmets, can sustain a g-force of 1200 with every slam of their head against a tree.[35] This would be like accelerating to 26,000 miles per hour and coming to a halt every second.[36] The speed of their pecking can be over six meters per second, and they may repeat the action over 12,000 times in a single day—all for the paltry prize of getting at an insect they hear burrowing deep within a tree.[37]

The mechanics that enable this are almost unbelievable in their design. One feature that helps protect the woodpecker is the size of its brain; because it is more compact, it is more durable; additionally, the

32. Estudio Arkano, "Your Mind Will Collapse," 4:33.
33. Loewen, "Football Concussions," para. 24.
34. Heintz et al., "Determinants," para. 2.
35. Field Museum, "Woodpeckers Show Signs," para. 1.
36. Cloud, "Woodpecker's Design," para. 19.
37. Cloud, "Woodpecker's Design," para. 19.

angle of the brain inside the skull and the snugness of the skull around the brain both prevent the brain from jostling much as the bird uses his head as a hammer.[38] Moreover, the bones that make up the skull are stiffer and stronger, with strategically placed spongy structures near the impact zones; the former distributes the impact of the hammering over a larger surface,[39] and the latter encases the brain like, well, a helmet![40] The bill of a woodpecker also aids in the protection of the bird: it has a slightly blunt tip that discourages the point from chipping off, and the two halves of the bill are slightly different lengths, allowing the bottom to hit the tree first, which sends more of the shock waves to the body rather than to the brain of the woodpecker.[41]

But the most bizarre design feature created to protect the woodpecker involves its tongue.

The tongue internally wraps around the bird's neck, constricting the blood flow to and from the brain, creating an excess of blood in the skull, which in turn creates a pressurized cushion of fluid around the brain.[42] Without these marvels of design, the woodpecker would undoubtedly suffer major brain injury or death. Interestingly, autopsies on woodpeckers reveal the presence of protein deposits that in humans do in fact indicate brain damage; in the woodpeckers, however, the protein deposits seem not to be evidence of damage but instead extra layers of protection against the force of their hammering.[43]

As if all of these are not enough to illustrate God's precision of design, add to them these facts: a woodpecker's feet are constructed like grappling hooks, with two clawed toes facing forward and two facing backwards, allowing a tenacious grip on the tree that enables the bird to align itself vertically with the tree; its tail feathers are especially stiff, and when the woodpecker presses them against the tree truck, they form a "tripod" for its body; both features align and stabilize the bird perfectly for its task at bill.[44] Finally, to protect the bird from the flume of sawdust that its drilling generates, spewing just a fraction of an inch from its face, God designed a third eyelid to

38. Cloud, "Woodpecker's Design," paras. 21–22.
39. McKittrick, "How Do Woodpeckers Avoid," para. 10.
40. Cloud, "Woodpecker's Design," paras. 21–22.
41. Phillipsen, "Woodpeckers," para. 55.
42. "How Much Wood," para. 2.
43. Field Museum, "Woodpeckers Show Signs," para. 6.
44. Phillipsen, "Woodpeckers," para. 13.

protect the bird's eyes and installed tiny tufts of feathers inside its smaller than usual nasal holes to prevent it from snorting the debris.[45]

Woodpeckers are a homey, familiar illustration of God's perfect design, evidence that God orchestrates even the smallest, most ordinary elements of nature. Design is conceivable and containable in something as small as a woodpecker, but when an even more intricate design is evident in huge, expansive elements of nature, it is beyond at least my human comprehension. Such is the case, again, in the cosmos. Although the cosmos is unfathomably large, as I have established, its order and design exist even at the cellular level.

As I pointed out in my preceding discussion of the cosmos, the observable universe is 150 trillion light-years in diameter, an aptly astronomical size that I personally cannot even imagine. Within that massive expanse lie millions of galaxies, of which the Milky Way is one. Within this galaxy, itself one hundred thousand light-years away, is situated our comparatively tiny planet earth, a paltry 13,000 kilometers in diameter. From out of the estimated 200 billion trillion stars, God chose one unassuming dwarf star, the sun, to be the one the earth orbits. Our moon, unlike the sun or the Milky Way—both of which are smaller specimens of stars and galaxies in the universe, respectively—is somewhat larger than most moons that exist in the universe.

In this tiny subsection of the universe, the earth's orbit around the sun is so huge that it takes 365 days to complete one orbit. To accomplish that task within a year, the earth has to move through space at over 67,000 miles per hour.[46] At the same time, the earth is spinning on its own axis, which tilts precisely at a 23.4 percent angle,[47] at a rate of one rotation per twenty-four hours, which sounds slow, but to make that one turn, it must spin at a rate of over 1,000 miles per hour.[48] This crazy combination of revolving and spinning is somewhat comparable to the Tilt-a-Whirl carnival ride, which shows up at every county fair. As your seat spins independently on a platform, the platform itself also rotates. Luckily, because of gravitational force, we do not have the same response to the earth's orbit or spin as we do to the Tilt-a-Whirl, or we'd have a constant mess to clean up. And if that's not enough spinning for you, the entire solar system is

45. Phillipsen, "Woodpeckers," para. 57.
46. Onwujiarri, "18 Amazing Facts," para. 15.
47. Jehovah's Witnesses. "Living Planet," para. 12.
48. Onwujiarri, "18 Amazing Facts," para. 13.

orbiting the Milky Way at about 447,000 miles per hour, and the Milky Way itself is moving through the universe.[49]

Why, out of all the vastness of creation's acreage, is the earth situated where it is in the Milky Way galaxy? Why is the earth exactly 93 million miles away from the sun in an elliptical orbit so minutely regular that the earth expands its distance from the sun only 1.5 *centimeters* per year, perhaps since the dawn of time?[50] Why this tilt, this speed of rotation and revolution? These specifications are so marvelously orchestrated and the interaction between them is so stunningly in harmony that it requires a high level of willful ignorance to think that even one of these factors could have been random or accidental. There is no question that our placement in space offers unequivocal evidence of a master designer's hand in the creation of the world.

Scientists universally agree that the earth's specific location in the Milky Way galaxy is beyond fortuitous. It is, as they refer to it, a "habitable zone" that provides the perfect combination of factors to allow life to exist on earth. If our orbit of the sun were even fractionally closer to the sun, or if it veered significantly from its elliptical course, the shape of which maintains a perfect consistency of distance from the sun,[51] we would incinerate—any further, we would freeze into people popsicles. Likewise, if our orbit of the sun was wavering or erratic, our days and nights would be unbalanced, resulting in extended length of days or nights that would also result in flame or freeze.[52]

Relatively speaking, however, the earth is nevertheless close enough to the sun that the sun could instantly annihilate its tagalong child. For example, the sun is over one hundred times bigger than the earth, and it regularly erupts with solar flares, massive, molten globs that tear away from the sun's surface and spew into space. These solar flares are not just interesting volcanic-like eruptions—each one has more energy and destructive power than billions of hydrogen bombs.[53] Similarly, the earth is susceptible to bombardment by enormous meteorites that regularly hurtle through space and form radiation that could poison and kill the planet, yet neither of these have ever proven any real threat to the earth because

---

49. Wendel, "How Fast," paras. 8–9.
50. Siegel, "Earth Is Drifting Away," para. 13.
51. Onwujiarri, "18 Amazing Facts," para. 8.
52. Britt, "13 Incredible," para. 4.
53. Jehovah's Witnesses. "Living Planet," para. 15.

of the double layer of protection that surrounds it. One protective layer is earth's atmosphere, a blanket of oxygen sixty miles thick that envelopes the planet. Given the vastness of what lies beyond it, the atmosphere is exceedingly thin, yet meteors that stray into the atmosphere are incinerated upon contact, converting them from missiles of mass destruction to lovely falling stars that we eagerly search for on August nights during the Perseids showers.[54] The atmosphere also absorbs harmful UV rays. Protecting earth from the sun's eruptions, meteors, and radiation, as well as a host of other potential dangers, is the earth's second defense—its magnetic field, which repels these outside attacks. These two features exist not only as protective elements, however; the atmosphere also conducts light and heat safely, and both it and earth's magnetic field stabilize temperatures on earth, keeping the planet within moderate zones.[55]

To these exquisitely designed elements, the moon and the earth's tilt are lovely lagniappes that God provided to complete his creation. The moon, especially because of its larger-than-average size, almost single-handedly regulates the ocean's tides, pulling them in and out multiple times per day, a washing agitation cycle that renews and refreshes earth's water supply; without such cleansing tides, the oceans would become stagnant and foul, robbing the earth of its precious and necessary supply of life-sustaining water. In addition, the moon affects the tilt of the earth, which is not a design *flaw* but an underappreciated genius of design. Many people, for example, believe that seasonal change is produced by variations in our distance from the sun, but it is actually the tilt of the earth that is responsible for temperature fluctuation,[56] for when, in its orbit, the tilt of the earth angles the Western Hemisphere away from the sun, that hemisphere experiences fall and winter; when the tilt exposes the Western Hemisphere more fully to the sun, it is spring and summer.

How are we to interpret the amazing coalescence of so many factors that enables life on earth—seemingly the *only* complex life that exists in the entire universe? The documentary *The Privileged Planet* enumerates the necessary elements that enable and sustain life on earth, which begins with liquid water, possible only because the earth is exactly the right distance from the sun.[57] If it were 5 percent closer, the sun would burn up the

---

54. Onwujiarri, "18 Amazing Facts."
55. Britt, "13 Incredible," para. 6; Onwujiarri, "18 Amazing Facts," paras. 4, 5, 7.
56. Jehovah's Witnesses. "Living Planet," para. 12.
57. USAHavana, "Privileged Planet," 15:03.

planet;[58] if it were 20 percent closer, carbon dioxide clouds would build up and freeze the planet.[59] The other factors that make life possible on earth include an orbit around a main sequence C2 dwarf star, protection by gas giant planets, a larger-than-usual moon, an oxygen-rich planet, correct mass of the earth, a magnetic field, the presence of plate tectonics, being within a circumstellar galactic habitable zone, a correct ratio of liquid water to continents, and a terrestrial planet.[60]

The scientists interviewed for the film uniformly agreed that given the vastness of the universe and the scarceness of conditions that would allow for these elements, the odds of all these factors being present are infinitesimally minute.[61] Yet they *have* coalesced, in the case of the earth. The film presents two dichotomous ways of interpreting our position in the universe, given these facts. To explain the two positions, they go back to Copernicus's radical hypothesis, which, against the prevailing belief of the time, suggested that the earth revolves around the sun rather than the sun revolving around the earth. This theory, which obviously dethroned earth from being the center of the universe, led several of the scientists in the documentary to regard the earth as just one of billions of specks in the universe, not set apart or special in any way. However, the same fact led Copernicus to consider our planet especially favored. Because he started with the premise of an intelligent designer, he rejected the idea that the earth is one of billions of insignificant specks on the universe, but instead believed that God privileged the earth, making it unique among the billions of entities in space. By contrast, though the scientists in the documentary were clearly in awe of the "against all odds" convergence of the previous list of factors, some nevertheless repeated the words *luck*, *chance*, or *fluke* rather than the word *God*.[62] It seems to me, however, that the focus of both camps is a bit askew, for both concluded that the earth, and by extension, mankind, were accorded a privileged position because of their uniqueness. The true purpose of the earth's distinctiveness, however, is not to exalt mankind's significance, but to illustrate God's awesome aptitude as the creator of the universe.[63]

---

58. USAHavana, "Privileged Planet," 16:48.
59. USAHavana, "Privileged Planet," 16:58.
60. USAHavana, "Privileged Planet," 21:39.
61. USAHavana, "Privileged Planet," 22:39.
62. USAHavana, "Privileged Planet," 25:50.
63. USAHavana, "Privileged Planet."

For me, there is no question about how to interpret the enormity and design of the universe. When I research and ponder the scope of the universe, I feel very much out of my element, which is land-based and limited. My head spins with its magnitude, as though, internally at least, I experience the disorienting whirl of the earth as it spins on its axis. God's creative capacity is so infinitely beyond ours in every respect that we should always feel humbled and awed. It is a proper position to bow with the psalmist and to declare our gratitude: "When I consider your heavens, the work of your fingers, the moon and the stars which you have set in place, what is mankind, that you are mindful of them; human beings, that you care for them?" (Ps 8:3–4)

Yet I do not believe that God wanted our response to his creativity to be entirely sober, nor do I think that he wants to intimidate us by his perfection. Another characteristic of God's creativity that assures me of these claims is the obvious *joy* he had in the creative process. This encourages me to see God in a different light—as fun-loving and even occasionally quirky. This is not, of course, a view that the Bible explicitly promotes: it may be in fact rather difficult to imagine the God of the Bible or even his human manifestation as Christ as joyful or joking or, frankly, even to picture either as *smiling*. By reverse logic, though, knowing God made us in his image and that *humans* are playful; love laughter, jokes, and surprises; and often indulge in fun-loving activities, it does not seem heretical to me at all to argue that these traits must also be part of who God is. Even though the Bible is silent in portraying God or Christ in these ways, his creation robustly manifests his quirky, playful, fun-loving spirit.

As evidence, I submit the platypus. When British explorers returned to England from Australia and Tasmania with a taxidermy specimen of a platypus, their audience was convinced that the animal was a hoax—a trick of taxidermy involving stitching elements of several animals into a single specimen,[64] a joke akin to the more modern day jackalopes that parents taking their kids on their first Western vacation alert them to keep an eye open for. If God created the animal kingdom and had a box of leftover parts with which to construct one last animal, the platypus would be the result. It defies most of the carefully organized categories that enable most species to be successfully classified. For example, it is a mammal, yet it lays eggs like a turtle rather than giving birth to live young. It divides its

---

64. Animalogic, "Platypus," 4:50.

time between being a land and an aquatic animal.[65] It has extra shoulder bones that no other animal has.[66] It has the furry body and the webbed feet of an otter, the bill of a duck, limbs on its sides like a reptile, the electrolocation ability of a shark, the venom of a snake, a tail like a beaver's, and an absence of teeth like an echidna (the spiny anteater, the only other animal in the species *Monotreme*).[67]

God not only had fun with designing the platypus' appearance but in assigning it skills and attributes as well. For example, it uses its tail not only for propulsion, but also to carry objects, in the same way a monkey uses its tail. The webbing on its hands and feet is longer than its fingers, so the extra webbing flaps like deflated rubber toys. It has no stomach,[68] and when viewed under a UV light, its fur glows green and blue.[69] It has poor eyesight and little ability to smell, so it hunts with its nose and eyes shut, depending wholly on its electrolocation skills.[70] In short, the platypus offers empirical evidence of God's sense of humor, and perhaps even suggests his delight in confounding our efforts to categorize his creation.

Even if the platypus wins the overall title of World's Quirkiest Animal, almost unlimited further examples of God's joy in creation exist in other animals' appearance, mannerisms, or abilities. For example, the Nicobar pigeon is a vulture-shaped bird with outrageous plumage. Bright blue feathers cover its underbody, and iridescent green feathers cover its back and shoulders. But what really sets the Nicobar pigeon apart from its drab, ledge-strutting city cousins is its head gear. Its sleek head sharpens to a point, but from its neck, long streamers of multicolored feathers—blue, red, yellow, green, and orange—dangle from its neck in a display wild enough to make a punk rocker envious. The Nicobar's necklace is so ostentatious that you have to believe that this is just one illustration of so many in the universe of God's jubilant joy in experimenting with how unique he could make each element of his creation. It is as if God deliberately gave quirky appearances, traits, capabilities, and idiosyncrasies to some of his creation for the sheer enjoyment he received by doing so. Note the range of his creativity in the following examples that I have collected over the years:

65. Animalogic, "Platypus," 2:54.
66. Spencer, "Duck-Billed Platypus," para. 4.
67. Animalogic, "Platypus," 4:03.
68. Animalogic, "Platypus," 4:25.
69. CBC Kids News, "Platypus Just Got Weirder," para. 2.
70. Spencer, "Duck-Billed Platypus," para. 3.

GOD'S CREATIVITY

- One tiny jellyfish can, in ideal conditions, live forever. When it suffers any kind of trauma, it absorbs its tentacles into itself and sinks to the ocean floor, becoming a little pat of jelly. Within hours, though, it reproduces polyps, the form it had before adulthood, and begins another life cycle.[71]
- A snail called the sea pangolin, because it lives in volcanic vents in the Indian Ocean that can reach up to 750 degrees, has a shell made of iron that protects it from the heat. Equally weird is that the snail doesn't actually eat anything during its lifetime; it feeds off of the energy that it receives from bacteria that latch onto a gland in its body.[72]
- Even though a caterpillar, in its transformation into a butterfly, completely liquifies, the emerging butterfly has memories of its existence as a caterpillar.[73]
- The great frigatebird can stay aloft for over two months, not touching ground at all during this period. Scientists have discovered that they sleep in one-minute bursts while flying, somehow keeping one side of their brain alert to avoid collisions with other birds.[74]
- A blue whale's tongue can weigh up to 2.7 tons, heavier than an elephant, our largest land animal; its heart can weigh over 1,300 pounds in some cases.[75]
- Seagulls stomp on grassy surfaces, mimicking the vibrations caused by rain, in order to lure earthworms to the surface.[76]
- Sea sponges are considered animals because they share several characteristics with animals, such as having a skeleton made of collagen, adapting in size, and digesting food. Yet sponges have no heads, mouths, eyes, heart, lungs, or brain.[77]

---

71. Osterloff, "Immortal Jellyfish."
72. Daley, "Deep-Sea Snail," para. 2.
73. Mckenna, "Butterflies Remember Caterpillar Experiences."
74. VanHelder, "Scientists Finally Have Evidence."
75. "How Big Is Blue Whale's Tongue?," para. 1.
76. GrrlScientist, "Watch: This Brilliant Bird."
77. Gibbs, "Question of the Week."

- Although hippos can't swim or even float, they can sleep underwater. They hold their breath for over five minutes at a time, and then, without waking, they instinctively bob up to the surface, grab a breath of air, and sink back down.[78]

- Trees can communicate with each other through their roots and soil, even when miles apart, a system that researcher Suzanne Simard calls the Wood Wide Web. Trees seem to recognize other trees that are like them, and older trees give preferential treatment to younger trees in their midst. Trees can share nutrients with each other through their root systems, and when they feel threatened by insects or weeds, they can communicate with other trees to develop a protective secretion that repels the threat.[79]

- Albatrosses live for over fifty years, and they spend the first five or six years of their lives entirely in flight over the ocean, never touching ground.[80]

- A fish called a climbing gourami can live out of the water. Its gills can transition from sucking water to sucking air, and they can even climb out of the water and, by using their fins and tails like awkward legs, walk for a good distance.[81]

- Porcupines float.[82]

- The arteries of a blue whale are so huge that humans could swim through them, if they ever got the urge. Which I wouldn't.[83]

- The fieldfare thrush has an unusual way of revenging itself on its enemy: it flies above it and targets it with its built-in poop bomb. Once its missile coats a bird's feathers, the excrement often so damages the targets' feathers that they cannot fly, and sometimes they even die.[84]

- A giraffe cleans its eyes and ears with its tongue.[85]

78. "Hippo," para. 7.
79. Bertsch, "Can Trees and Animals?," paras. 4–5.
80. Warne, "Amazing Albatrosses," para 11.
81. See "Climbing Gourami."
82. "North American Porcupine," para. 4.
83. "Blue Whale's Heart," para. 6.
84. Mani, "Fieldfares Poop on Their Enemies," paras. 6–7.
85. Lovgren, "Animal Myths Busted," para. 1.

- A hippo's sweat is at first clear, but after exposure to air, it turns red. Scientists discovered that this change was caused by two molecules, which they cleverly named hipposudoric acid and norhipposudoric acid.[86]
- As if an octopus' eight limbs were not enough of a fun oddity, each of its tentacles has a tiny brain at the end of it that works in conjunction with its central brain. The octopus also has three hearts and blue blood.[87]
- Bamboo rarely blossoms, usually only once every 30 but up to 120 years! When a certain species does decide to flower, by silent command, every other stand of that species, no matter where it's located or what season it's in, will blossom at the same time. And then they die.[88]
- A reindeer's eyes adapt to the seasons by changing color. In winter they are blue, since they can absorb more of the less prevalent light, and in spring and summer they revert to a brownish hue.[89]

Obviously, to expound only upon the bountiful beauty, deep design, extravagant excess, and jubilant joy of God's creativity presents only some of the features of God's boundless creativity. Other qualities, like goodness, truth, and originality, are intrinsic to his creativity as well. And, though we cannot achieve the level of creative excellence that God possesses, he has endowed us *all* with the ability to express creativity in some way and calls us to demonstrate the same qualities in our art as he does in his. A proper understanding of human creativity would be to regard it as an affirmation of God's creation, an act of worship that emphasizes not our own ability, but gratitude to God for sharing his artistic flair with us. As Evie Shaffer puts it, "our making is an outward expression of the internal work of God's life-giving breath on us."[90]

This is certainly the view that the Bible espouses, celebrating both God's and our creative capacities. Scripture especially honors God's first recorded attribute—creativity—as a primary and pervasive aspect of his being, permeating nearly all his actions. Some of my favorite biblical

86. Kean, "Sweating Blood," para. 8.
87. "9 Brains, 3 Hearts," paras. 5–7.
88. "Why Do All Bamboo Trees," answer by Aamir Khan.
89. Fosbury and Jeffery, "Reindeer Eyes Seasonally Adapt."
90. Shaffer, "Creative's Role," para. 10.

passages are the ones that acknowledge God's creativity by characterizing him as an actual artist plying the materials of art. One of the better-known examples is Isa 64:8, which imagines God as a sculptor and we, as at Adam's inception, as the clay in his hands: "We are the clay, you are the potter; we are all the work of your hand." A similar verse is Heb 12:2, in which God is a writer, forming our faith as an author creates a book with language—"looking unto Jesus the author and finisher of our faith" (King James Version). In both passages, the materials that God as artist works with are we. We humans, the only element of creation made in the image of God, are blessed to be the art objects that God continues to shape and revise, for "we are God's handiwork, created in Christ Jesus to do good works, which God prepared in advance for us to do" (Eph 2:10).

The full range of God's creativity should not go unnoticed by his people. The Bible is full of verses expressing awed praise for his artistic finesse, displayed in the gallery of nature. In Eccl 3:11, the speaker declares that "He has made everything beautiful in its time. He has also set eternity in the human heart; yet no one can fathom what God has done from beginning to end." Though this verse juxtaposes the magnitude of God's creativity with human limitation, it also affirms that "he has set eternity in the human heart," a clause that acknowledges our God-given, intrinsic belief in and desire for life beyond this one, life that lasts and that we can aspire to. Amos focuses on God's creative nature as the principal way he demonstrates his power and almighty nature, describing God as "He who forms the mountains, who creates the wind, and reveals his thoughts to mankind, who turns dawn to darkness, and treads on the heights of the earth—the Lord God Almighty is his name" (4:13). This verse, like the one prior, also focuses on the gap between God's artistry and humans'—his scope is beyond ours ("he forms the mountains"; he "treads on the heights"), his creativity is nebulous to us, beyond our understanding ("who creates the wind"), and all-encompassing ("who turns dawn to darkness"). Yet again, the phrase stating that God "reveals his thoughts to mankind" reiterates our partnership with God and our access to his truths, satisfying the human hunger for higher thoughts and expressions.

The Psalms especially exalt the creativity of God. Psalm 104 is entirely dedicated to enumerating the glories of creation and joyfully confirms God's continuous involvement in nature's re-creation and restoration: "When you send your spirit, they are created, and you renew the face of the ground" (104:30). Isaiah 45 records God himself announcing his creative sovereignty, authorizing the elements of nature to be the instruments of his righteousness and salvation: "I form the light and create darkness . . . You heavens above, rain down my righteousness; let the clouds shower it down. Let the earth open wide, let salvation spring up, let righteousness flourish with it; I, the Lord, have created it" (vv. 7–8).

To me, the most beautiful of the passages that celebrate God's creativity, however, are those that personify the elements of nature and depict them as praising their creator for their conception, a response that we ourselves should emulate. In Ps 19, David imagines creation exulting in the artistry that God demonstrated in fashioning it: "The heavens declare the glory of God; the skies proclaim the work of his hands. Day after day they pour forth speech; night after night they reveal knowledge. They have no speech, they use no words, no sound is heard from them. Yet their voice goes out into all the earth, their words to the ends of the world" (vv. 1–3).

Though I love this image of insentient nature voicing praise, it is, of course, only an imaginative portrayal of an act that only we humans are actually privileged to perform. Only to humans did God give the mental capacity to respond in this way to their maker; only to humans did he give the gift of language and the ability to discern and express meaning in the world. In short, only we humans were created in the image of God himself. The implications of this fact are staggering and almost impossible for us to fully comprehend. Part of what this means, though, is that many of the traits that God possesses we also possess, and that only we, out of all creation, have souls that are capable of seeking relationship with God, souls that are eternal and have the potential for endless existence in the presence of God. *Imago dei* means that because God is creative, we also are endowed with creativity—*all* of us, whether we recognize, admit, or practice it or not. *Imago dei* is a gracious gift, but also a serious responsibility, a dual calling that I will explore in the next chapter.

2

Emulating God: The Command to Create

IMAGO DEI. MADE IN the image of God. Our God-given purpose in life is to nurture in ourselves the attributes of God that he instilled in us in embryonic form. As if to emphasize that creativity would be a foundational way we emulate him, God chose to form mankind as an artist would a sculpture, molding clay into tangible form. Yet he then went far beyond what any other artist could do with his or her art: he breathed life into that sculpture, making it an animate being, moving from soil to soul, equipped in that moment to participate with God in the ongoing work of creation. Madeleine L'Engle comments beautifully on this fact by pointing out the etymology of our material origin: "The root word of *humble* and *human* is the same: *humus: earth.* We are dust. We are created; it is God who made us and not we ourselves. But we were made to be cocreators with our maker."[1] How astounding it is that despite our humble origins and the unworthiness it connotes, that God chose to share his nature with us and to endow us with perfect, untainted creativity! From the very beginning, for example, God allowed Adam and Eve nearly carte blanche to express their creativity. Their roles, as given in Gen 1:28 and 2:15, 19–20, were to care for the garden, to name its animals, and to reproduce to populate the world. Because caring for the garden originally entailed nothing difficult that could be considered work as we would now define it, and because

---

1. L'Engle, *Walking on Water,* 157.

childbirth as yet involved no pain, we have every reason to believe that Adam and Eve delighted in all three of these creative roles.[2] And, as Geoff Gentry points out, all three of these roles were explicitly creative in nature.[3] Caring for the garden gave them the right not only to maintain it but to reorder and even improve it; naming the animals invited them to create language, inventing words to uniquely identify a huge variety of life forms. And the most personal, unique, and pleasurable creative opportunity given to them was to create children in their own image, as well as in God's! This last creative mandate, as Lockerbie points out, is one that all creation is capable of, but only humans can reproduce other beings made in God's image.[4] Gentry notes that Adam and Eve were not limited to *only* these activities, of course, but were also encouraged to worship God and to respond to the beauty of what he created.[5]

Gentry expounds upon God's original command to "be fruitful and multiply," arguing that God's desire for Adam and Eve—and for us—"extends beyond human reproduction: we should multiply the world by creating something new from materials already there."[6] This insight underscores the priority that God placed upon human creativity from the beginning. God not only gave us permission to create, but he *commanded* us to do so, out of his deep desire for us to truly develop the creative potential he has given us. Unfortunately, just as the fall damaged God's original plan for humanity, so has it broken our originally perfect ability to create. However, if we continue to nurture and express our creative impulses, striving to realize as much as possible the full range of our potential in an effort to emulate God, God can use our efforts to redeem us. As one of my students, Caleb Gammons, beautifully put it in a discussion board response, "Human creativity is God's image stubbornly, powerfully, beautifully shining through the brokenness of humanity and this world. Someday, in the new and redeemed creation, our image-bearing will be perfectly free from sin. Then all will create because God creates, just like everyone will be kind as God is kind or everyone will love as God loves. Creating is not merely a discipline but truly part of who we are. The discipline of it is not the creativity itself, but the work required to draw the creativity out of our sinful selves."

2. Lockerbie, *Timeless Moment*, 19.
3. Gentry, "Theology of Making."
4. Lockerbie, *Timeless Moment*, 19.
5. Lockerbie, *Timeless Moment*, 19.
6. Lockerbie, *Timeless Moment*, 19.

Most Christians would not question that we should devote ourselves to growing in love, compassion, mercy, fairness, patience, and so on—all attributes originating in God that humans, because we are made in his image, have the capacity to express as well. Yet fewer acknowledge that God also calls us to emulate his creativity. The logic in neglecting the call to creativity is usually that God has gifted only certain individuals with creativity. Those with an artistic bent should develop their talent, they might argue, but not everyone has the capacity for creativity; this latter group is exempt from growing in creativity, for you can't express what you don't possess.

But no. *Imago dei* means that God endows each of us with *all* his communicable traits, though our sinful natures prevent us from fully realizing them as they are realized in God. Only God's incommunicable traits—those that set him apart as God, traits such as his omniscience, omnipotence, omnipresence, and eternal existence—are beyond our human capacity to possess. God is a creator, and we are made in his image, so all humans have the capacity to create.[7]

Part of our resistance to the call to be creative may be our fear of so great a gift, a gift with immeasurable power. L'Engle suggests, for example, that "we are afraid of that which we cannot control; so we continue to draw in the boundaries around us, to limit ourselves to what we can know and understand. Thus we lost our human calling because we do not dare to be creators, co-creators with God."[8] A more pervasive explanation for our resistance to my claim of universal creativity is that our definition of creativity is far too narrow, for most of us, when we think of creativity, tend to limit it to the arts. Creativity, in this view, is equated with the ability to do such things as to draw or paint, to be musically or theatrically inclined, or to be skillful with language. Creativity does, of course, include the arts, but to limit it to only these expressions restricts its scope and keeps us from recognizing our own creativity in a multitude of other areas. For example, when I ask my students to raise their hands if they consider themselves to be creative, only perhaps one fourth respond that they are. But when I point out the grace and skill involved in a football receiver leaping for a ball, their feet instinctively staying within the field of play; or note the imagination in a mathematician's exploration of the infinite patterns of fractals, uncovering design amid chaos; or marvel at a teacher's ingenuity and persistence in constructing an individually adapted learning program

---

7. Terry and Lister, *Images and Idols*, 50.
8. L'Engle, *Walking on Water*, 191.

for a mentally challenged student, they begin to see that creativity is much more expansive than they think.

Defining creativity more broadly came up as a topic in a recent conversation I had with my two sisters. I had just told them of the upcoming launch of my new book that my university was hosting. My younger sister Teresa commented that I "was given all the artistic ability in the family." By contrast, she depicted herself as "not having a creative bone in my body." Our older sister Beth, she pointed out, could play the piano beautifully and has the patience and skill to do cross-stitch and crochet. I can draw, write, and create crafts. Because she felt untalented in any of these areas, my younger sister considered herself uncreative. But as we three continued to converse, both my older sister and I agreed that one area of our younger sister's creativity lay in her ability to organize and plan—a talent that is not usually classified as creative. However, creativity can display itself in any activity that engages your imagination or prods you to explore beauty or order or design. Gardening, meditation, baking, losing yourself in a sunrise, washing the dishes, reading a book—literally anything can be a creative outlet if it's seen from the right perspective or done with the right attitude. If you think it's a stretch to regard washing the dishes as having creative potential, you've not read Anne Voskamp's *One Thousand Gifts*; in that book, washing the dishes induces rumination that leads to spiritual insight and serves as the impetus for a lovely, imaginative description of soap bubbles. And, in that same vein, I'd argue that a second unusual area of creativity that my younger sister excels in is laundry—she knows all the techniques in getting stains out and is passionate and persistent in her efforts and imaginative in her methodologies. Are these not traits of an artist?

In my research for this book, I came across many lovely, expansive definitions that helped me have a wider view of what creativity can be. One of the broadest definitions I found was one offered by Shawna Scafe: "Anytime[sic] you take an idea and use your abilities to make it a physical reality, you are creating."[9] This definition does not focus on skill, talent, or even necessarily imagination or originality—only a successful effort to transform something imagined or thought of into tangible form. Another source defined it simply as "being intentionally curious,"[10] a definition I love because it highlights the value of a key trait that motivates and generates creativity; the word *intentionally* also stresses the initiative we must take in discovering more about

9. Scafe, "Christian Women," para. 4.
10. "Simple Tips," para. 6.

the areas that pique our curiosity. Three other definitions emphasize the importance of originality in what we create: "the ability to bring something original and valuable into the world,"[11] *Oxford English Dictionary*'s "relating to or involving the use of the imagination or original idea to create something," and "creating something unique out of what already exists."[12] With so many ideas already explored and so many works of art produced by artists more talented than most of us, a common response to such definitions is to question whether it is possible to produce something truly new or unique anymore. My answer—and God's, I believe—is yes! No one has ever had your unique perspective, your particular style, or just your method of organizing, presenting, or fashioning, for your personal experience and personality inform all the above. C. S. Lewis adds this additional insight: "Even in literature and art, no man who bothers about originality will ever be original: whereas if you simply try to tell the truth (without caring two pence how often it has been told before) you will, nine times out of ten, become original without ever having noticed it."[13] As the third of these definitions makes clear, no one has God's *ex nihilo* ability, but our uniqueness as individuals assures that what we produce will be very different from what others may create, even if we were all given the same assignment.

Beyond originality and imagination, another element crucial to creativity mentioned in the first of these three definitions is reiterated in this one: "Creativity is the execution of an idea which has both originality and *value*"[14] (emphasis mine). Value, of course, has nothing necessarily to do with monetary worth or even with others' recognition of a creative effort as important or worthy. Instead, it means that the artists themselves produced something that they considered worthy of their time and that in creating the art they conveyed that idea, meaning, or message to an audience. Ultimately, it is God who assigns and recognizes value in what we create, so if as artist Christians we create art that expresses God's nature and produce it to honor him, we can be sure that our art has value.

One of my favorite definitions of creativity is the one posited by Norman Rosenthal, who defines creativity as "having the ability to make unexpected connections, either to see commonplace things in new ways—or unusual

---

11. Gaines, "Fostering Creativity," para. 7.
12. "How to Be," para. 22.
13. Lewis, *Mere Christianity*, 191.
14. Skillicorn, "What Is Creativity?"

things that escape the attention of others—and realize their importance."[15] This ability is precisely what Emily Dickinson identifies as the key attribute of poetic vision in her poem "This Was a Poet." In the poem, she parallels a poet's keen observation skills and ability to interpret and "[distill] amazing sense/From ordinary Meanings" (ll. 2–3) to an "attar," or a concentrated essence used to make perfume. The poet's creative ability, Dickinson claims, not only enables the rest of us to see common things, such as the "familiar species/That perished by the Door" (ll. 5–6) as uncommon and special but also has the power to discern meaning in the "ordinary" that others miss. Sharing their insight is like releasing a fragrant attar and its scent permeating those who attend to the poet's craft.[16]

When we define creativity in these freer, less restrictive ways, it enables us to acknowledge the truth that we all possess a measure of God's creative capacity. If we define creativity more broadly, we can acknowledge that creativity can also be manifested in raising vegetables, baking and cooking, relating to children, performing athletically, caring for animals, dancing, keeping records, planning vacations, finding shortcuts for tasks, or, yes, even organizing well. For, as far as we know, neither Adam nor Eve painted, played an instrument, wrote a book, or sculpted. Yet they practiced creativity, as I have already claimed, through naming the animals, tending Eden and later farming the land, and by reproducing children—God-given commands that they accomplished creatively.[17] We too can live our ordinary lives, fulfill our responsibilities, and do our work not dully or mindlessly, but with energy, imagination, and originality, and in so doing we're exercising another dimension of what God created us to be.[18]

Defining creativity this broadly may be the only way some people would be willing to identify themselves as creative, but I want to make a bolder claim: I believe that all human beings possess the ability to be creative in the arts as well. In other words, even if we use the narrower definition of creativity that usually comes to mind when we mention that word, as artistic aptitude in writing, painting, drawing, sculpture, crafts, music, theater, dance, fiber art, woodworking, needlework, and the like, I believe God endows all human beings with the aptitude and skill to express creativity in these areas as well. The explanation for why so many people do

15. Fuchs, "Creativity May Be Key," para. 3.
16. Dickinson, "This Was a Poet."
17. Terry and Lister, *Images and Idols*, 50.
18. Scafe, "Christian Women."

not evidence this type of creativity isn't because they don't possess potential for such work, but because they have not fully tested their aptitude or interest in these areas. It is not that God limits our access to artistic creativity by granting talent to just a few, but that we limit *ourselves* by our lack of effort or interest in exploring the full range of our creative potential. Some do not try their hand in any artistic area; others may make efforts in a few areas without experiencing, in their opinion, satisfactory results, and therefore conclude that they lack talent in the arts. But even in this much, much narrower way of defining creativity, there is still an incredible range of creative options available, a huge variety of artistic endeavors to explore, so the chances are great that those who consider themselves uncreative actually have just not yet discovered an area that might interest them or an area that corresponds to their talents and skills.

For example, in my own experience, which I will detail in the next chapter, I discovered a couple of artistic areas that interested me and in which I demonstrated a dim talent at an early age: writing and drawing. I dabbled in these media for years, improving only slightly in my skills due to my uneven commitment to them; it was only when I worked under a talented art teacher while in high school that my skills in that field took off, and my writing ability demonstrated the same improvement when I majored in English in college. These artistic interests were fulfilling enough for me that I explored no other outlets for my creativity. My 2021 New Year's resolution to consistently practice my creativity, however, morphed into a multitude of artistic areas, some of which had little or no resemblance to my established talents and none of which I intended, planned for, or foresaw. This experience convinced me of the truth of my claim above, however, that we all have the capacity for creativity in the arts, possibly in multiple areas.

As a qualifier to my claim, however, I am not suggesting that everyone has the same level of giftedness in the arts or equal amounts of talent, skills, or abilities in approaching them. Nor am I arguing that everyone has potential for success in any form of art they might choose. Without question, some people have amazing natural aptitude in certain artistic areas and can create beautiful works of art almost effortlessly; others, no matter how hard they try or how intrigued they are by the same area of art, cannot approach the mastery that God blessed this first group with. Yet it is also possible that the second group could excel at a different form of art that the first group could never master.

What I *am* claiming is that all people, if they devote enough time and effort to the task, can discover some area of the arts that interests them and for which they have an aptitude. The exploration and experimentation involved in finding that area would itself be an exercise in creativity, so it is a process I would urge everyone to consider. And, because I consider creativity in the arts a worthy and possible pursuit for anyone, this book will work under this assumption, using the arts as my primary illustration and context as I discuss creativity and encourage your participation in it.

When we recognize our own personal areas of creativity and commit to investing in our intrinsic creative natures, we can begin to live the creative lives that God wants for us. For our creativity and our real effort to develop it truly matter to God. His design was that every person's creativity would be a note in a beautiful symphony, and everyone's note is crucial to the composition. As Matt Tommey explains, "your creative 'language' uniquely represents God's voice on the earth and in the Spirit."[19] Scripture gives us directions for how to best practice our creativity and encourages us in our efforts. Ecclesiastes 9:10, for example, advises that "whatever your hand finds to do, do it with all your might." Colossians 3:23–24 reiterates this instruction and adds a specific motivation: "Whatever you do, work at it with all your heart, as working for the Lord, not for human masters, since you know that you will receive an inheritance from the Lord as a reward." Both of these passages stress the necessity of true devotion and sincere effort applied to the task, resulting in our best efforts. Romans 12:6–8 acknowledges the many unique areas of giftedness that exist and urges us to identify our individual strengths and interests. All these Scriptures confirm my point that we differ in *areas* and *levels* of creativity, but that we *all* have been given some gift to develop, while 1 Tim 4:14–15 challenges us to "not neglect [our] gifts" but to "give [ourselves] wholly to them, so that everyone may see [our] progress." This last clause—"so that everyone may see our progress"—hints at another motive for exercising our creativity: it can be a witness to the world, enabling them to see a glimpse of God. As Tommey puts it, our art is a "window to the heart of God designed for Him to flow His presence through in order to touch the lives of His people and change the earth."[20] Proverbs 22:29 encourages us to strive for excellence in all we do: "Do you see someone skilled in their work? They will serve before kings."

19. Tommey, *Unlocking the Heart*, Day 6.
20. Tommey, *Unlocking the Heart*, Day 6.

In my opinion, the Scripture that best explains the beautiful interplay between God's creative nature and our own, enabled by *imago dei*, is Eph 2:10, where the writer identifies humans as "God's handiwork." Lockerbie points out that the word translated as *handiwork* is the Greek word *poiema*, the word we translate as *poem*, so a more exact wording of this verse is that we are "God's poetry."[21] This word choice emphasizes that we ourselves are God's creative output, a beautiful poem he has written. Because we are created in God's image and share in his creativity, God's poem can beget poetry of its own, establishing a creative loop that pulls us back to God as our source and expands outward from him to produce our own creative work.

Our creativity, of course, as established earlier, will differ from God's in its imperfection and in its inability to create *ex nihilo*; we as his image bearers can only create something new from existing materials. In fact, Michael Card rightly points out that for us to believe that we are capable of *ex nihilo* creation or that our human creativity can approach God's perfection would be akin to our "acting like little gods, creating on our own in the same way God creates."[22] To stymie this arrogant stance, J. R. R. Tolkien referred to humans as sub-creators, a term that acknowledges that our creativity is derived from God yet is not a license to consider ourselves God-like in our powers. Conversely, the qualities of God's creativity—beauty, design, extravagant excess, and joy—explored in the previous chapter are accessible to all of us, and each should be apparent in our creativity as they are in God's. For example, all artists, I think, aspire to express beauty through their art, and Christians should pronounce this intent even more distinctly. Moreover, we should align our definition of beauty with God's—beauty that conveys his nature. This is not to say that our art should only reflect an aesthetically pleasing view of the world, for suffering, pain, and even sin are realities that can be the legitimate subjects of art; in these cases, the beauty of the art may be in its truthfulness, in that we accurately represent God's view of our subject matter. The realities themselves may not be beautiful, but the redemptive purpose we convey through our art is.

For example, in creating the story of the prodigal son, Jesus depicts the son's debauchery using specific and raw language, naming his sins of drunkenness and sexual promiscuity. Jesus' choice to add the detail of the son's temptation to eat the filthy husks he is feeding the pigs he tends

---

21. Lockerbie, *Timeless Moment*, 31.
22. Card, *Scribbling in the Sand*, 28.

would have been especially repugnant to his audience. They would have regarded pigs as nonkosher and therefore repulsive in and of themselves, but to degrade oneself further by eating the putrid swill reserved for such animals would have been a graphic image of human depravity. The scene Jesus painted, then, is sordid and ugly, a true and stark picture of sin; the story, however, is beautiful in its juxtaposition of this ugliness with the unconditional forgiveness and restoration offered by the father.

Our art should also engage the other facets of God's creativity. For example, it should reflect design, both in its composition and in the purpose and meaning it expresses. As I clarified with regard to beauty, our art's purpose may be to reflect the disorder and chaos evident in the world, but if it further reveals that chaos to be a result of departure from God's design, the purpose and meaning of our art can still reflect beauty, truth, and design. Further, though the scope of our art cannot, of course, approach the extravagant excess that God displays in his creation, we should nevertheless think big, attempting to stretch our imaginations well beyond human vision, to use the full gamut of creation as inspiration for our own work, to refuse limitations on what our art can be or what it should look like. At the same time, we should also think small, attending to the minute but profligate detail that can also give us endless subject matter for our art. And, of course, our creativity should bring us pleasure as it does for God—God wants us to *enjoy* practicing our art, to allow it to enrich our lives. Creativity should never feel like a burden or chore, but an expression of our pleasure in emulating God.

We need to understand the fullness of *imago dei*, that God has given us the capacity for all God's communicable traits. If we accept this, we cannot claim that creativity is a trait that God gives only to some. Nor can we regard creativity as just an option to develop. God wants all of us to develop our full potential as humans, to not neglect any aspect of the *imago dei* that he gives us. As Harold Best points out, "biblically speaking, the making of art [exercising our creativity] is not an option but a command."[23] This expectation is not a burden, a demand on our time or one more obligation to fulfill that adds to our stress. Rather, it is part of God's plan for us, enabling a fullness of being, giving expression to our full potential, the complete range of who God created us to be. As Joel Clarkson so aptly expresses it, creativity takes faith out of our heads and puts it into our hands. We are not just the sum of our intelligence, so Descartes's assertion "I think; therefore I am" is inadequate to

---

23. Quoted in Card, *Scribbling in the Sand*, 12.

describe our identities. And by developing more and more areas of the *imago dei*, we begin to know more intimately the character of God, and thereby enhance our relationship with him.[24] This is only one of many benefits of committing to a regular practice of creativity, a truth that my own experience illustrates, a story I will relate in the next chapter.

---

24. Clarkson, "How Creativity Connects Us."

3

Committing to Creativity and Maintaining an Artistic Mindset

Even as a young girl, I was drawn to a creative life. I loved to draw, and Christmases and birthdays brought me Jon Gnagy paint sets, sketch pads, and one time, an easel, which I set up in the yard to draw from nature, as I had seen artists on television doing. I felt so artsy and professional, lacking only a beret and a paint-daubed smock. Craft time was my favorite time at VBS, and I later entered art contests, displayed my work in 4H, and took art all four years of high school, which increased my skills tremendously. Even more pronounced was my interest in writing. I spent hours in my treehouse with a pad of paper and a pen, producing an assortment of sappy, metrically awkward poems; unfinished, derivative "novels"; and overwrought short stories. However, my sixth-grade teacher saw a glint of talent in my work and would often post my assigned paragraph on her bulletin board, a recognition that stoked my motivation, and after winning a prize or two in church-sponsored contests, I began to form my career goal; I told everyone who asked that I wanted to be a Semi-Famous Small Town Author: successful enough to be known, but not so famous that I would have to live a City Life, making appearances and having my everyday existence uninterrupted by autograph requests and unsolicited photographs.

    I kept these interests throughout college, majoring in English education, and I continued to value the arts as I moved into married life, high school teaching, parenthood, graduate school, and through my career as an English professor. Other than writing my master's thesis and my dissertation and other mandatory papers in my graduate classes, however, I wrote nothing during those years, and even more neglected were my art talents. Despite my lack of literary and artistic production, however, I retained a strong interest in both. I roamed the aisles at Hobby Lobby, drooling over the paint kits, beautiful papers, and marker sets, and I collected supplies I loved to look at but didn't use. I also built up a collection of beautiful journals that I didn't write in. I became borderline obsessed with *Pinterest*, and through scrolling through it, I acquired a strong interest in altered books, yet despite creating multiple boards of ideas to use and buying supplies to create some, I never actually started making one. Mentally, I had made it into a daunting task, a project requiring hours of time I didn't think I had available.

Years passed in this pattern. My interest in creativity didn't wane; in fact, my desire to write and produce art increased yearly, yet I rarely acted on my desire. Though during this span of around twenty-five years my creativity remained mostly fallow, I did have one spurt of writing activity that produced a crop. Fueled by my discovery and love of Annie Dillard's work and by a sabbatical that provided a semester off to devote to writing, I produced an academic book of literary analysis on her creative nonfiction: *Annie Dillard and the Word Made Flesh: An Incarnational Theory of Language.* It was my first published book, a lifelong dream come true. I can still remember the euphoria of receiving the letter that informed me that they had decided to publish my book and the tearful ride to campus, so grateful that God had affirmed my efforts and talent by giving me the opportunity to be published.

Incredibly, though, instead of this being an impetus to keep in Writing Mode, over ten years passed before I began working on another book project, this time a book I wrote during blocks of time chipped from a slightly lighter teaching load in 2020. This second book—*Reentering Eden: Christian Meditation in Nature*—was not aimed at an academic audience, but rather a Christian lay audience, a wholly new direction for me. By the end of the year, I had completed it, yet the hard work of finding a publisher for it, a process that involved researching compatible presses, filling out multiple publication applications, composing market analyses, cover letters, synopses, surveys of comparative books and annotated tables of content, and choosing sample chapters to send was intimidating enough to keep me from taking definitive steps towards its publication.

Again, I mentally defeated myself, convincing myself that I was too busy or not talented enough, telling myself that my one publication was a fluke that I couldn't hope to repeat. I grew more and more frustrated with my resistance, because at some deeper level of myself, I believed I had talent that I was squandering through my inactivity and undermining through my self-deprecation of the abilities God had given me. These recognitions added guilt to my frustration, making me more miserable and angry with myself, yet instead of providing the necessary impetus to take action, they ironically increased my resistance.

Finally, however, my frustration swelled to a breaking point, a level I could no longer live with or make excuses for, so on New Year's Day in 2021, I made a resolution designed to make it as easy as possible for me to move from my stasis. Instead of identifying a specific focus for my creative efforts or naming a particular project that I wanted to complete, I purposely worded my resolution vaguely and determined only to do "something creative" every day. Making my resolution general to the point of generic gave my goal flexibility and opened up more expansive possibilities for the directions my creativity could take. With this loosely defined goal, I hoped to avoid the intimidation that looming, time-intensive projects had evoked in me in the past. I went into the new year hopeful but only guardedly optimistic that that year would be different than my previous aborted attempts. Because the previous failures still lurked in my memory, an edge of self-doubt remained. Yet this time, almost miraculously, my resolution held and grew feet, and the consistent practice that I established that year transformed creativity into a habit that literally has changed my life in ways I couldn't have imagined.

My first artistic foray was starting an altered book. I chose this as my starting point because it was an artistic project that had intrigued me for a few years. I reasoned that if I began with an area of art that was completely new to me, that the freshness of the medium and the excitement of experimentation would energize me and infuse my efforts with some of the same power.

I was right. Fueled by the excitement of trying something new and my efforts made easier by the sizeable collection of art supplies I had accumulated over the years, the first bleak days of January filled with my creative efforts. Very soon, working on a single book seemed too limiting, so I began work on several theme-centered altered books simultaneously: one focused on nature, another on quirky humor, and another on

Scripture and spiritual wisdom. This variety kept my work stimulating and allowed me more options for pages to create.

Less than three weeks of renewed—and consistent—creativity was enough to kindle the glowing embers of my creativity into a small but steadily burning fire, enough flame to prod me to finally finish that project that had intimidated me for so long: initiating a publication search for the book I had finished. For a while, the intensity of this chore usurped my more enjoyable creative experimentation with which I had started the year, so I tucked in projects when I found the time that kept the search for a publisher from dousing the flame.

By the end of February, I had hit the mark of time that usually converts a desire into a habit, and I felt more confident that I had begun something that would last. Looking over my two months of creative output, I realized that practicing my creativity regularly had increased my skills—my initial efforts at calligraphy, for example, were awkward and disjointed, but as I studied and practiced different styles, I acquired my own, and my lettering became more fluid and graceful. In addition, I found that as I tentatively began creating very simple altered book pages, my imagination expanded: ideas multiplied for using different media, adding texture, design, and embellishments, and experimenting with different layouts. Best of all, my heightened creativity was not limited to my altered book pages. Within a month, I had found a publisher for my book, and with this success, my other writing flourished, replenishing my nearly dried up well of topics and quickening the currents of my writing process.

Happily, my renewed commitment to creativity also fostered my experimentation in several areas that were completely new to me. By the end of the year, I found myself looking, shocked but smiling, at my Moleskine planner with check marks in most squares, indicating that I had succeeded in doing "something creative" nearly every day, and the "something" had taken far more forms than I could have imagined. In the course of that year, I had replaced the flooring substructure of my cabin and had laid laminate flooring in my cabin and in the kitchen and foyer of our home as well. I made a bench out of an old door and an enclosed bookshelf with another, produced hundreds of framed calligraphy quotations on old dictionary pages, made Christmas decorations from Mason jars, produced signs lettered onto barn siding and planed slices of trees, made mug shelving from an antique suitcase, constructed a footstool and a small table from piles of old books and wood slabs, wrote and submitted three articles to a magazine, and completed a large drawing that I had begun several years ago but had abandoned. The number of things I produced and their variety bolstered my confidence and increased my range of skills. Best of all, my creativity wasn't simply functional or just an exercise in aesthetics; it also became a spiritual experience, due in part to the research on nature I conducted for my writing and the quotes and Scriptures I artistically presented in my altered books and calligraphy, but also because engaging my creativity felt like worship, a way to express gratitude to the ultimate Maker. Because my primary motive for increasing my creativity was to nurture and develop an aspect of *imago dei* that I had neglected, I believe that God especially blessed my efforts.

Though God's blessing is the most likely explanation for the expansion of my creativity, research reveals that certain qualities and attributes especially foster creativity, some of which I possessed. Tanner Christensen offers a list of eight personal traits that "cause" creativity, a list that I have adapted and expanded for my discussion here.[1] There are two important points I want to emphasize about these attributes. The first is that these need not be, and in fact rarely are, intrinsic traits of creative people. We can *acquire*, deliberately pursue, and cultivate every one of them, adopt them all to develop our creative potential. The second point is that no one person possesses perfectly all the traits that contribute to creativity or lives a life in which beauty and truth—ideally byproducts of a creative life—are consistently valued. Time and time again, as I read about the lives of creative people, I discovered gaps or absences, even major moral failings, in every person I studied. In one respect, this is encouraging, for it assures us we need not be perfect to live out our *imago dei* creativity; on the other hand, it is a discouraging reminder of how rare it is for humans to *abide* in the image of God. Therefore, because it is impossible to find a perfect exemplar of all the creative attributes, I use a variety of creatives to illustrate my points, though I will particularly emphasize Annie Dillard. This will be my approach in chapter 5 as well, where I will use Flannery O'Connor as my focus.

Christensen opens his list with the attribute of confidence, which he defines as the "ability to question without fear."[2] Confidence also involves believing in your abilities and having the bravery to take initiative. It is true, as Henri Matisse pointed out, that "creativity takes courage,"[3] for it

---

1. Christensen, "What Causes Creativity?"
2. Christensen, "What Causes Creativity?"
3. Leith, *Symbols in Life and Art*, 29.

is intimidating to begin with a blank page or canvas and to trust that you can produce something worth keeping, a feeling Paul Cezanne knew well, for in a statement often attributed to him, he said, "It's so fine and yet so terrible," he confessed, "to stand in front of a blank canvas." Dillard adds the fact that not only beginning a new piece but continuing to work on one in progress requires an equal amount of courage: "As the work grows, it gets harder to control; it is a lion growing in strength. You must visit it every day and reassert your mastery over it. If you skip a day, you are, quite rightly, afraid to open the door to its room. You enter its room with bravura, holding a chair at the thing and shouting, 'Simba!'"[4] Vincent Van Gogh possessed a more pronounced schism between self-doubt and belief in his abilities than does Dillard, yet hopeful confidence in his talent usually won out, as is evident in this letter to his brother Theo: "I feel such a creative force in me. I'm convinced that there will be a time when I will make something good every day, on a regular basis. I'm doing my very best to make every effort because I am longing so much to make beautiful things. But beautiful things mean painstaking work, disappointment and perseverance."[5] The courage and confidence to overcome the trepidation of creation are not often innate impulses. We may have to actively resist self-deprecation, insecurity, and doubt. We must believe what God already knows about us—that we have more inside of us than may be evident on the outside—a truth vividly illustrated by these affirming facts recorded in the devotional based on Dan McCollam's writing, *All about Releasing Creativity*.[6] Our lungs, if laid out, would cover as much area as a tennis court. Our nerves, if laid out in a single line, would extend forty-five miles. Our circulatory system would travel much further, however, wrapping a veiny trail around the earth two and a half times, or 60,000 miles. Most impressive, though, is the extent of our DNA. If it were possible to lay the strands of our DNA end to end, the 6.5 foot length that is in every one of our 37.2 trillion cells would stretch from earth to the sun and back *seventy times*. The magnitude of our DNA is symbolically significant, for our DNA is responsible for our individual identities, the unique characteristics that make us who we are. Our bodies are literally packed with our uniqueness. Every cell of our body proclaims our distinctiveness, an individuality that receives expression through our art. Our internal "bigness," according to

---

4. Dillard, *Writing Life*, 52.
5. Van Gogh, "Letter 09/09/1882," para. 5.
6. McCollam, *All about Releasing Creativity*, Day 4.

Raynor, is why we can create art that is greater than ourselves.[7] Add to that the fact that we as believers have the mind of Christ and that our bodies serve as residences for the Holy Spirit and we begin to have a sense of how immensely valuable we are to God; keeping this in mind should help us keep self-doubt at bay. As Christians, of course, we are keenly aware that we owe our uniqueness to God and that we can only create because God's power enables us. I read somewhere that the Catholic novelist Walker Percy, before he began any new book, used to offer the simple yet honest prayer, "Lord, I am beginning with nothing. Help me." Though I've not been able to confirm that attribution, I admire the humility and recommend the posture before God it advocates.

A mindset that especially impedes courage is perfectionism, a tendency I incessantly battle against. For many years, I considered my perfectionism an asset, since it often resulted in higher quality end products, from grades to goals. The problem was, though, that my perfectionism also kept me from attempting things new to me, since I was unwilling to try anything that might yield less-than-perfect outcomes. Thus, my too high self-expectations severely restricted my creative output because perfectionism does not allow for error; a perfectionist mindset considers anything less than ideal output as a failure. This is the paradox of perfectionism: because it demands flawless work, it often results in our accomplishing no work at all; the fear of failure paralyzes us from even attempting to create. The only way to entirely avoid failure, however, is to do nothing at all, which is, of course, the ultimate failure. We must, as Jon Acuff stresses, "be brave enough to be bad at something new," a daunting but necessary attitude.[8]

Thus, a better mindset to have, one that curtails perfectionism and develops self-confidence, is humility, another trait Tanner Christensen identifies as encouraging creativity.[9] It might seem paradoxical to argue that humility increases self-confidence, yet if we can accept our imperfections and limitations, it is easier to admit the fact that we will sometimes create junk, and this humility allows for lowered self-expectations and a willingness to fail and be vulnerable. Creating requires bravery, being willing to fail and to be vulnerable. Just as we mature more through our trials and struggles than through trouble-free days, so creativity develops best when we allow mistakes to develop us rather than discourage us. Edison famously

7. Raynor, *Bezalel*.
8. Acuff, "Be Brave Enough," 6:01.
9. Christensen, "What Causes Creativity?"

said, "I have not failed. I've just found ten thousand ways that won't work." Every mistake takes us closer to producing an ideal, so I'm working on not being frustrated when things go wrong in the process, but to see each error or unsuccessful effort as a necessary step in the path towards creation. As Zig Zigler wisely points out, "Mistakes are proof that you are trying,"[10] and James Joyce purportedly claims even more for the value of making mistakes, insisting that "mistakes are the portals of discovery." Since I have adopted this mindset, I have quit berating myself (as often!) for failures, and I also spend less time trying to "fix" my errors in order to avoid starting over on a project. Sometimes it's just easier—and best—to wad up a draft or tear out a page of an altered book or paint over a flop. Such an attitude regards imperfect work, failures, and mistakes as necessary and ultimately useful steps in the process of creativity, since discovering what does *not* work enables us to better recognize what does. Regarding creativity as a trial-and-error process rather than the construction of a masterpiece can free you to be more experimental in your approach.

Alternately, we can choose to look at the "mistake" differently and consider the possibility that botches can become beauty. This, I think, is what Scott Adams has in mind when he claims that "creativity is allowing oneself to make mistakes. Art is knowing which ones to keep."[11] A crafter whose blog I read said she keeps all the baby wipes she uses to mop up drips, clean her brushes, or wipe off her hands so that she can later integrate them into her artwork; her practice demonstrates her conviction that she looks for beauty in what others would consider disposable. Sometimes, what at first looks like something that has ruined my artistic effort becomes the impetus for trying something new. For example, instead of starting over when I spilled watercolor onto a page, I intentionally added spills of different colors, creating a more interesting backdrop for an altered page. Other "errors" have pushed me to experiment with including different layers or media in my altered books or to choose an entirely fresh metaphor as a guiding principle in a piece I was writing. To quote Bob Ross's most famous saying, "We don't make mistakes, just happy accidents."[12]

With my writing, I also came to accept some truths about drafts. As Jodi Picoult, a prolific modern writer, states, "You can always edit a

---

10. Ziglar, "Mistakes Are Proof . . ."
11. Adams, *Stick to Drawing Comics*, 347.
12. Quoted in Haun, "Happy Accidents," para. 10.

bad page. You can't edit a blank page."[13] Further, most published authors also seem to agree with Anne Lamott, who claims that "almost all good writing begins with terrible first efforts. You need to start somewhere."[14] This perspective corresponds with John Dufresne's idea that "the purpose of the first draft is not to get it right, but to get it written."[15] Ultimately, I had to accept that "[not] all the things we make are good, but it ... is good that we are making things,"[16] and acknowledging the truth of this was instrumental in restoring value to my flawed drafts, enabling me to lower my self-expectations and recognize that it would be more productive to consider drafts, as well as all my other artistic efforts, as valuable *practice*. This is a difficult mildest to adopt, because all writers have a vision of what they want to offer the world—meaningful concepts beautifully expressed in language—yet they recognize the truth of Tasha Alexander's lament that "once you start writing, the book immediately loses all its shiny goodness. Instead of the theoretical perfection it was in your head, it becomes what every writer recognizes—a first draft."[17] Even Annie Dillard, whose writing contains such lovely, lucid language that it seems to have escaped such a disappointing transition from mind to page, admits that she too regularly experiences the discrepancy between vision and execution. "[The draft's] relationship to the vision that impelled it is the relationship between any energy and any work, anything unchanging to anything temporal.... You try—you try every time—to reproduce the vision, to let your light so shine before men. But you can only come along with your bushel and hide it."[18] This disconnect between vision and reality, authorial intent and audience reception, seems to be at the heart of Dillard's self-doubt. In *The Writing Life*, Dillard recalls writing the essay "Transfiguration" and her concern that she might be separating herself from her audience.

> I was too far removed from the world. My work was too obscure, too symbolic, too intellectual. It was not available to people. Recently I had published a complex narrative essay about a moth's flying into a candle which no one had understood but a Yale critic,

13. Youngling, "You Can't Edit," para. 1.
14. Myers, "Almost All," para. 1.
15. "Here's Why," para. 2.
16. Gentry, "Theology of Making," para. 17.
17. Sugarek, "Interview," para. 3.
18. Dillard, *Writing Life*, 58.

and he had understood it exactly. I myself was trained as a critic. I was a critic writing for critics: was this what I had in mind?"[19]

Her thoughts are interrupted by a visit from two very young boys, who begin asking her questions about the essay, having obviously read it. Encouraged by their interest in the story and their enjoyment of it, Dillard seems ready to exchange her self-doubt for pride, prompted by her hope that even these young boys could access the depth of her intent; however, she is abruptly returned to humility when one asks, "'Did you *write* that story? . . . Or did you type it?'"[20]

Perfectionism, self-deprecation and self-doubt, and fear of failure are all adult inhibitions that arguably all stem from pride. It is arrogance that leads us to tolerate no failure, to insist that being perfect is somehow possible for us. Pride makes the creative process all about *us*, as creators, not about the art itself or about the one who gave us our talents and skills, for we are consumed with how "bad art" might reflect negatively on us and our abilities. Adopting a more humble stance towards our work dismantles our pride and opens us to a less demanding and me-centered approach to our art.

Another trait that fosters creativity is attentiveness, or what Tanner Christensen calls "observation."[21] As Emily Dickinson states in the poem cited in the last chapter, a poet not only notices the "familiar species" that often escapes our ordinary attention but ponders its significance as well. If we have such intentional attentiveness to the world, our art will benefit, for, as James Broughton is said to have stated, "the only limits are, as always, those of vision"; the keener our vision, the fewer limitations upon our art. Yehudi Menuhin, the virtuoso violinist, identifies this trait, with its attendant "awe, wonder, curiosity, exaltation, humility" as "the very foundation of any real civilization," a state of being that every human should possess and nurture, so integral is it to fostering creativity. Applying its value to his own field of music, Menuhin comments that "to be an outstanding musician, you have to be very attentive to the smallest detail and willing to have infinite patience in the pursuit."[22] Whereas Menuhin's emphasis is on attention to harmony, tone, and precision of notes and their timing, Vincent Van Gogh, who received most of the inspiration for

---

19. Dillard, *Writing Life*, 54–55.
20. Dillard, *Writing Life*, 56.
21. Christensen, "What Causes Creativity."
22. "Yehudi Menuhin Quotes."

his work from nature, often spoke of the necessity of attentiveness to the natural world: writing to his brother Theo, Van Gogh assured him that despite his poverty, he had everything he needed to continue his artistic life: "I . . . have nature and art and poetry, and if that isn't enough, what is?" Earlier in the letter, he had encouraged his artistic brother to have the same focus: "Always continue walking a lot and loving nature, for that's the real way to learn to understand art better and better. Painters understand nature and love it, and teach us to see . . . Find things beautiful as much as you can, most people find too little beautiful."[23]

Such a focus offers unlimited material to an artist, for a truly creative person understands that even the smallest element of nature can be an impetus for art, as was the case with Pablo Picasso, who is said to have stated, "The artist is a receptacle for emotions that come from all over the place: from the sky, from the earth, from a scrap of paper, from a passing shape, from a spider's web." Attentiveness to detail and the ability to convey to her readers the awe and wonder she herself feels toward the minutiae of nature is one of Annie Dillard's greatest strengths. In one of my favorite quotations from Dillard, she reiterates Picasso's valuation of observation when she writes, "Our life is a faint tracing on the surface of mystery, like the idle curved tunnels of leaf miners on the face of a leaf. We must somehow take a wider view, look at the whole landscape, really see it, and describe what's going on here. Then we can at least wail the right question into the swaddling band of darkness, or, if it comes to that, choir the proper praise."[24]

Pilgrim at Tinker Creek is replete with evidence of Dillard's sensual awareness: she stalks a muskrat, examines pond water under a microscope, marvels over the shadows of clouds reflected—or not—in Tinker Creek, and sniffs the delicate scent of honeysuckle transmitted by a butterfly's fanning wings. Although Dillard herself is far more attentive than most of us could claim for ourselves, still she admits her inadequacy compared to the attentiveness—spurred by curiosity—of children through a story she relates of a walk with a young child. The story relates her effort to see a caddis fly case; despite her diligence and sincere searching, however, she is unable to find a specimen in the wild. However, while walking casually with a young girl, appropriately named Sally Moore, not she, but the little girl quite nonchalantly notices a case and asks Dillard what it is.[25] Her story illustrates

23. Van Gogh Museum, "Letter to Theo van Gogh," paras. 8, 3.
24. Dillard, *Pilgrim*, 9.
25. Dillard, *Pilgrim*, 90.

not only the rewards of attentiveness, but also makes the point that children are more intuitively attuned to the landscape. This is because children more commonly embody curiosity and wonder, traits that we as adults allow to atrophy as we age. It seems foolish or childish to adults to express unrestrained delight in the details of the world, but children give full vent to their delight. Likewise, adults sometimes consider joyful play as an immature waste of time, but as Scafe argues, we need to reclaim these childlike impulses, for they enable the most original, expressive forms of creativity.[26] Madeleine L'Engle references Finley Eversole's findings that point out that at the age of five, 90 percent of children measure as possessing "high creativity," but by age seven, only 10 percent have retained that level of creativity. By adulthood, Eversole claims, only 2 percent can be classified as highly creative.[27] L'Engle urges the necessity of retaining a childlike spirit when she writes, "In the act of creativity, the artist lets go the self-control which he normally clings to and is open to riding the wind. Something almost always happens to startle us during the act of creating, but not unless we let go our adult intellectual control and become as open as little children."[28] I truly believe this is one attribute of children Jesus had in mind when he told his disciples that "unless you change and become like little children, you will never enter the kingdom of heaven" (Matt 18:3), for only those who actively seek and joyfully receive are given a glimpse of heaven. For, unlike most adults, who over time allow their once-innate attentiveness to the miraculous beauty and variety of nature to fade, children daily enlarge their capacity for wonder by giving full reign to their curiosity and delight. What to adults is regarded as ordinary and unremarkable—for example, a common wildflower or a gust of wind—to a child, are delightful surprises, found treasures, captivating enough to merit their full attention. Children will stoop to pick the flower so they can examine it more closely; they will also run to show it to their parents because their delight is too big to hold within themselves. A gust of wind becomes a playmate that inflates their coat sleeves and invokes giggles. They will dance with the breeze, bowing their head to it to allow it to tickle their scalp and tousle their hair, whereas an adult will likely draw his jacket more tightly against his body to shut out the winter's chill. The world is wonder-full to children. Their curiosity makes exploration and experimentation common impulses that do not lose

26. Scafe, "Christian Women," para. 11.
27. L'Engle, *Walking on Water*, 77.
28. L'Engle, *Walking on Water*, 81.

force with use, but instead feed their imaginations and expand their wonder. That is why we would do well to consider the truth of a comment attributed to Tim Burton that "anybody with artistic ambitions is always trying to reconnect with the way they saw things as a child." Creativity thrives and multiplies when we allow wonder, curiosity, imagination, attentiveness, and delight to play freely and run in all directions. As Hans Rookmaker rightly points out, "Freedom is the necessary basis for creativity, for creativity is impossible when there is timidity, when you allow yourself to be bound by narrow rules."[29] These attributes, like creativity itself, are also part of God's nature, qualities that account for the exuberant profusion that is so evident in creation, qualities that explain the blue bills of boobies, the waddle walk of penguins, the wild blue and yellow plumage of a Nicobar pigeon. How can we argue that God himself does not revel in imagination, curiosity, delight, wonder, and play? And why do we believe that it is proper and wise to crush these impulses in ourselves as we grow past childhood?

Christensen identifies *mindfulness* as another attribute that encourages creativity; he defines the term as "thinking on how to think," a sort of metacognition that to me suggests the ability to adapt your mind to novel situations, to have a mental malleability that allows an imaginative response to all experiences.[30] A. J. Cropley is said to have put it this way: "The creative thinker is flexible and adaptable and prepared to rearrange his thinking." Edmund Burke is alleged to have said that "there is a boundary to men's passions when they act from feelings, but none when they are under the influence of imagination." It is telling that even Albert Einstein, who most of us would more readily align with intelligence, fact, and scientific thought, degrades all these and instead privileges imagination. "I am enough of an artist," he is said to have written, "to draw freely upon my imagination. Imagination is more important than knowledge. Knowledge is limited. Imagination encircles the world. . . . Logic will get you from A to B. Imagination will take you everywhere."

As the repetition of the word in the quotations above shows, perhaps no other quality is more associated with creativity than imagination. In fact, most people regard creativity as synonymous with imagination. And, just as observation intertwines with curiosity, each dependent on the other for existence, so is imagination inextricable from originality and uniqueness. A jaded response to originality, as I noted in the last chapter, would

29. Card, *Scribbling in the Sand*, 137.
30. Christensen, "What Causes Creativity?"

be to argue that originality, in the purest sense, is impossible, that every thought has been expressed, every idea has been formulated; this is the position of the world-weary, disillusioned speaker of Ecclesiastes, when he sighs that "What has been will be again. What has been done will be done again. There is nothing new under the sun" (1:9).

But I would argue that all creativity is original, by virtue of the fact that every one of us, by God's design, is unique, unlike any other person. Every semester when I introduce my students to College Composition, I assure them that what they write will be original because no one else has exactly their style, their voice, their ideas, and their stories. I would assume that most of the ideas, inventions, beliefs, or methods we identify as original and unique have a predecessor to us—before we came up with the idea, someone somewhere probably formulated the same idea, invention, belief, or method that we consider original to us, but as long as we are unaware of those previous ideas when we imagine our own, our ideas or inventions are original. For example, some years ago I was pondering the tea bag. I envied the portability and ease that tea drinkers had in using the bags to enjoy a freshly brewed cup of tea. I wondered why no one had ever considered marketing coffee bags for those of us who hate tea but love coffee. A few years after that, I noticed coffee bags for sale at a grocery store. Could I have sued that inventor for stealing my original idea? No, because the idea was original to both of us—and probably several hundred more—but only one person acted upon his or her creativity. Sadly for me, as Henry Ward Beecher is said to have proclaimed, "the ability to convert ideas to things is the secret of outward success." Curses.

Imagination and originality are traits especially pronounced in Annie Dillard's work. She practically invented the genre of creative nonfiction, or at least is largely responsible for its dramatic increase in popularity. Her influence upon the genre is uncontested. Apparently, she was blessed with this attribute early on, for in *An American Childhood* she imaginatively re-creates an early memory of a curious monster that illuminates her bedroom, sliding across the walls, crouching behind furniture. Eventually, she recognizes the monster as the cars that pause at a stop sign on her street before turning in different directions, their headlights flashing into her room as they move.[31]

---

31. Dillard, *American Childhood*, 20–21.

Another facet of imagination or originality is resourcefulness, which Christensen clarifies as "something to tinker with."[32] To me, the word suggests the ability to use available materials to put them to new uses. Richard Dean Anderson made a career out of this concept when he played MacGyver in the TV show of the same name. MacGyver's special skill was to rig up some kind of gizmo week after week that would save him or someone else from being blown to bits, lost in Antarctica, or buried alive, using only materials at hand, like matches, a wad of string, a handy magnet, or static electricity produced by rubbing his sweater. This show took literally Frank Lloyd Wright's lovely definition of an idea: "An idea is salvation by imagination."

My mom, besides being creative in so many conventional ways—sewing, baking, flower gardening, writing, decorating cakes—was gifted with resourcefulness as well. For example, to cheer the dreariness of my windowless basement bedroom, she hung a window pane on my wall, backed it with a magazine picture of a sunny outdoor scene, and hung a florescent light behind it. She converted a useless abandoned chest freezer into a greenhouse to start her tomato and pepper plants, using the original hanging wire baskets as drip trays and a sheet of Visqueen as a cover.

As important as all these traits are to creativity, however, every one of them is worthless unless we back it up with initiative. As was clear by my brilliant idea to market coffee bags, creativity is ineffectual unless we enact, put to use, or realize it. Maybe I could have become a millionaire, or perhaps coffee bags could have made me famous, right up there with the guy who invented cup sleeves to protect our hands from Starbucks' burns or the person who decided we needed fidget toys. But I missed my opportunity when I kept my brilliance at a concept level, where it could benefit no one.

Curses.

Therefore, energy—a dedication to creativity and persistence in pursuing it—and action—not just thinking about creativity but doing it—are perhaps the most important traits we can possess in order for our creativity to have purpose and usefulness. Christensen addresses this necessary facet in his final two creativity traits, energy and action.[33] Dan McCollam adds to this, stressing the sober responsibility we have as Christians to steward well the gift we have been given, pointing out that "ideas and innovations that are not acted on forfeit their God given authority to shape and influence

---

32. Christensen, "What Causes Creativity?"
33. Christensen, "What Causes Creativity."

culture." We should not, they argue, regard creativity as being at the mercy of inspiration, something we must wait for, but see it instead as a force within us that is our responsibility to "stir up."[34] Similarly, James Russell Lowell is said to have wisely commented that "creativity is not the finding of a thing, but the making something out of it after it is found." Arnold Glasow is credited with being much blunter: "An idea not coupled with action will never get any bigger than the brain cell it occupied."

Quite obviously, the people we revere as creative geniuses possess this trait, or they would have produced no work for us to admire. Early in his career, Handel produced a cantata *weekly* for the church at which he was the music minister; later in his life he accomplished an even greater feat. Commissioned to compose a libretto for a charity benefit, he accepted the commission but estimated that it would take him a year to complete. Instead, in a frenzy of productivity, during which he barely left his home or took the time to eat, he finished the 260-page score in only twenty-four days—and gave *Messiah* to the world. "I did think I did see Heaven before me, and the great God himself," Handel commented later.[35] Vincent Van Gogh displayed a similar dedication to his art; in a time when most artists played to the market, producing a popular subject that would sell well and allow them to support themselves for long periods of time without producing more art, Van Gogh remained true to his own aesthetic and worked continually to improve his painting skills.[36] Flannery O'Connor was also dedicated to her craft. Despite increasing debilitation from lupus, O'Connor set aside every morning for a writing session. Even when she was hospitalized, knowing that her death was imminent, she smuggled in drafts of the last story she was working on, "Parker's Back," intent on finishing it before she died.[37]

Dillard also demonstrated discipline and adhered to a strict schedule of work. A schedule, she writes, "defends from chaos and whim. It is a net for catching days. It is a scaffolding on which a worker can stand and labor with both hands at sections of time. A schedule is a mock-up of reason and order—willed, faked, and so brought into being; it is a peace and a haven set into the wreck of time."[38] She lived out this dedication, spending

---

34. McCollam, *All about Releasing Creativity*, Day 1.
35. "Leo Frideric Handel," para. 12.
36. "Vincent Van Gogh."
37. O'Connor, *Habit of Being*, 585.
38. Dillard, *Writing Life*, 32.

evenings alone in the Hollins College library after hours, writing *Pilgrim* from the stacks of index cards which contained her voluminous notes. Dillard produced nearly every book after that point in an equally dedicated way—for example, she wrote *Holy the Firm* from an unheated yard barn in the Pacific Northwest. In that book, she uses the story of a moth that fell into her candle's flame as a metaphor for the dedication an author must demonstrate towards her work. Like the moth, Dillard claims, an author should sacrifice herself to the flame of her inspiration in order to provide illumination to her readers. "She burned for two hours without changing, without bending or leaning—only glowing within, like a building fire glimpsed through silhouetted walls, like a hollow saint, like a flame-faced virgin gone to God, while I read by her light, kindled."[39] This is a Christ-like posture she challenges her students to adopt as well: "How many of you, I asked the people in my class, which of you want to give your lives and be writers? . . . And then I tried to tell them what the choice must mean: you can't be anything else. You must go at your life with a broadax. . . . They had no idea what I was saying."[40]

Though it took me longer than these creatives to dedicate myself in such a way to my creativity, an awareness of the worth of such a commitment finally gave me the impetus to turn desire into discipline. I finally realized that I had to make small but deliberate efforts towards the larger goals I had; with Van Gogh, I began to see that "great things are done by a series of small things brought together," a quote attributed to the great painter. In my case, procrastination was less of an obstacle than my drive towards perfectionism. I was afraid to start if I couldn't do well, but now my motto is "done is better than perfect," and a quotation that has helped me to be consistent and productive is this wisdom attributed to Marie Forbes: "The key to success is to start before you are ready." My perfectionism was preventing me from *ever* feeling ready, and I had to fight off my instincts in order to replace perfectionism with a humility that allowed space for weak efforts, failed drafts, and dry periods with little inspiration. Steve Chandler even urges us that "the cure for writer's block . . . is to go ahead and write badly . . . Once you are in action, it's easy to pick up the energy and pick up the quality."[41]

---

39. Dillard, *Holy the Firm*, 17.
40. Dillard, *Holy the Firm*, 18.
41. Chandler, *100 Ways to Motivate Yourself*, 158.

As you were reading this chapter, I hope you were evaluating your own characteristics against these attributes that encourage and develop creativity, crediting yourself with the traits you already possess and challenging yourself to work on the areas that are not naturally part of your make up. Because you chose to pick up this book on creativity in the first place, chances are that you possess more of these characteristics than you lack. I, for example, was strong in attentiveness and curiosity, and maybe a little too humble, to the point that I doubted my abilities. I felt I had the potential to be imaginative and original, at least in spurts, but my perfectionism squelched my confidence to such a degree that though I had the energy and the desire to create, I rarely acted upon that desire.

Now that I'm approaching three years into a strong and consistent commitment to practicing my creativity, I believe I am stronger in all these areas. Creativity begets creativity, of course, and, as I have nurtured and developed my creativity, I have come to realize that it is an intrinsic part of my identity, something I now *need* in order to feel complete. "The discipline of creation," Madeleine L'Engle wrote, "be it to paint, compose, write, is an effort toward wholeness,"[42] and in trying to emulate my creator, I am finding that fullness.

---

42. L'Engle, *Walking on Water*, 74.

4

The Benefits of Creativity

As Christians, it should be our heart's desire to be more like God—to love his attributes and want to emulate him as much as possible. This is not always easy, of course, since he is wholly good and we are not. Yet if we love him, his goodness should appeal to us more than anything of the world. Romans 12:2 is a good statement of how we should live our lives. "Do not conform to the pattern of this world, but be transformed by the renewing of your mind. Then you will be able to test and approve what God's will is—his good, pleasing, and perfect will."

This Scripture supplies such a rich interplay of contrasts and causal relationships: first, the verse sets up a distinct contrast between the world's interests and God's standards, values, and ways of living. Paul alludes to the world's *patterns*, which suggests to me the predictability of how the world operates and thus the ease with which we can lose our own special individuality and find ourselves following a worn path that everyone else is walking. *Conform*, the world's value, is contrasted with God's value of *transform*; *con-* as a prefix means "with" or "together," but *trans-* means "across" or "to the other side of," making it clear that God has something very different to offer us on his side—not a life of mindless regularity or imitation, but a life of change, a life on "the other side of" the world's. The verse even tells us how this is effected—through the *renewing* of our *minds*. A life with God requires that we have a new way of thinking, a way that does not care how or what the world thinks but instead is drawn to the mind of Christ. When we allow our thinking to move to "the other side," we find ourselves suddenly cradled in the will of God, which, because it is God's, can be nothing but "good, pleasing, and perfect." "Now we have received, not the spirit of the world, but the Spirit who is from God, that we might know the things that have been fully given to us by God" (1 Cor 2:12).

Nothing evil, nothing detrimental, nothing even disappointing can result from our seeking to emulate God: only the "good, pleasing, and perfect," only the Spirit capitalized in our lives. Every attribute of God's that we try to emulate—including creativity—can only result in benefit to our lives, and because God our Creator loves and values every aspect of who we are—our bodily selves, our minds and emotions, our souls that house his Spirit, that *imago dei* within each of us—those benefits flood every aspect of our beings, even aspects we'd expect to be unaffected by creativity. Amazingly, for example, being creative can even fight disease. According to Maria Cohut, creative activity, notably writing, can increase your lymphocytes, cells that boost your immunity, and even just listening to music can bolster your immune system.[1] Creativity, especially activities like playing an instrument or acting, also helps develop both hemispheres of the brain, which results in better cognitive function, improving our problem-solving abilities and memory.[2] The brain stimulation that results from practicing creativity also extends mental sharpness into old age.[3]

Another important physical benefit of practicing creativity is a longer life span, influenced by a mindset of "openness to experience."[4] "Openness," as defined by a study published in the *Journal of Aging and Health*, involves "cognitive flexibility and the willingness to entertain novel ideas," and the study concluded that only openness *that is the result of creativity* contributes to longer life. Researchers explained this correlation by pointing out creativity's tendency to activate multiple brain networks, a stimulation that exercises the brain and keeps it supple.[5] For example, creativity improves problem-solving ability through its capacity to come at an issue from multiple angles instead of limiting problem solving to a linear, logical approach. Because of their more flexible way of viewing problems, creative people are also more adaptable to uncertain situations.[6]

1. Cohut, "What Are the Health Benefits?," paras. 27–28, 31.
2. Cohut, "What Are the Health Benefits?," paras. 21–24.
3. Fuchs, "Creativity May Be Key."
4. Gaines, "Fostering Creativity," para. 3.
5. Rodriguez, "Creativity Predicts," para. 3.
6. Carver, "Why Creativity Is So Important," para. 4.

Creativity's benefits to the brain also result in several mental or emotional benefits. Studies have shown that creative activity releases endorphins, the "feel good" hormones that improve mood and promote happiness. Osho, an Indian philosopher, clarifies the connection between creativity and joy when he allegedly wrote, "You can be creative only if you love life enough that you want to embrace its beauty, you want to bring a little more music to it, a little more dance to it."

This is perhaps the most significant mental benefit of creativity—its ability to positively affect mental health.[7] The *American Journal of Public Health* examined over one hundred studies on the effects of creativity and concluded that creative activity has an undeniable positive effect on mental health. Those who practice creativity reported that they felt fewer negative emotions and more positive emotions and that they felt less stressed, anxious, or depressed when they devoted time to creativity. In fact, even when their creative activity was random and unplanned and even when their history of creative practice was limited, one study found that creativity still produced all these positive mental effects. Perhaps best of all, benefits were noticeable even when creative sessions were only forty-five minutes long.[8] These benefits may be due to the fact that creativity provides a distraction from stressors[9] or because creativity offers an outlet for expressing difficult-to-articulate emotions that, if kept pent-up and repressed, could contribute to depression, anxiety, or stress. In a study of older adults in a nursing home that exhibited depressive symptoms, the researchers found that when the subjects were offered a variety of creative outlets, they demonstrated lessened depressive tendencies and acquired a higher level of self-esteem.[10] Another study involving adolescents found that when they were offered group art therapy, their self-concepts improved, they became more aware of their emotions, they felt less lonely, they had improved interactions with their peers, and they experienced improved self-confidence, a wealth of benefits from a single creative endeavor.[11]

This last effect, increased self-confidence, is an especially pronounced benefit of creativity. Again, only forty-five minutes of creative practice is necessary to produce, in some cases, radical results: creative

7. Cohut, "What Are the Health Benefits?," paras. 8–17, esp. 14–15.
8. Frank, "Study Says Making Art," paras. 4, 6.
9. "5 Big Benefits," para. 23.
10. Ching-Teng et al., "Positive Effects of Art Therapy," abstract.
11. Huang et al., "Effects of Group Art Therapy," abstract.

practice boosts self-confidence by up to 73 percent![12] The productivity, increased skill acquisition, and enlarged boldness and risk-taking that result from regular creative practice all contribute to this dramatic increase in self-confidence.[13] As James Clear points out, consistent practice, and the self-confidence gained through it, have the greatest influence in moving a person from doubting his or her creative potential to being convinced of its viability in their lives.[14]

This was certainly the case in my experience. As I branched out in my creative practice, I began experimenting in areas in which I had no background or expertise, and as I successfully accomplished one task, I found myself growing more confident in my abilities and more willing to tackle new projects. For example, I started a relatively small repair of my cabin floor, intending just to replace a square of flooring that had been badly compromised by a stubborn woodchuck that insisted on living under my cabin, but I ended up replacing the entire floor. After this major project, I ambitiously decided to install vinyl plank flooring above it. The project was easier than I expected and so fulfilling that my confidence was boosted enough to prompt multiple follow-up projects: laying laminate in my house's foyer and kitchen, installing new faucets in two bathrooms, rehanging my cabin door so it swung outward, even tearing down a section of our deck, bolstering it with concrete footings and braces for a new fish pond, and laying new deck boards. Now, my first impulse when something needs fixed, replaced, or redesigned is to look for a YouTube video explaining the process to see if I think I can do it myself. Though there are several areas beyond my pay scale, I definitely have increased my range of skills and my confidence level exponentially.

A final mental benefit of creativity is the increased focus it enables. The concentration required to work on a creative project and the sustained attention it takes to complete an artistic work are factors that contribute to honing focus.[15] In this respect, creativity becomes a meditative experience, for it evokes a single-mindedness of purpose that yields satisfaction, pleasure, and contentment.[16]

12. "5 Big Benefits," para. 11.
13. TeachThought Staff, "Significant Benefits."
14. Clear, "Creativity."
15. "5 Big Benefits."
16. Patel, "Five Incredible Benefits," para. 9.

THE BENEFITS OF CREATIVITY

I have no idea whether practicing creativity has ever increased my levels of CD4+ lymphocytes, but I can attest to experiencing many of the other physical and mental benefits that I've outlined here, and I can attribute all of them to the influence of creativity. When I committed to making creativity an integral part of my life, I almost immediately began to reap the benefits of that new focus. I had previously depended on crossword puzzles, Sudoku, and other word games as ways to remain mentally sharp—they were enjoyable pastimes, but ultimately, they felt trivial and a waste of time to me. When I began using that time to produce art or to take on new challenges instead, I noticed that these activities exercised my mind far more than my earlier pursuits; more importantly, *creating* felt like a more worthy use of my time. I had artistic creation rather than completed puzzles to show for my time investment, and my life felt more purposeful. I looked forward to the times I could devote to creativity, energized by my increasing skill and the challenge and excitement of trying new media, collecting ideas for further projects, and simply having time to myself to nurture a neglected aspect of my *imago dei*. Every new page in an altered book, every new décor item I constructed to add to my office or cabin, every new creative nonfiction piece I began, revised, or finished added to my satisfaction, self-confidence, and joy. My leisure time is now productive, and now the peace, self-confidence, mental sharpness, and imagination that all my research promised as rewards for creative practice did, in fact, flood in to replace the frustration I used to feel when I did not make time to develop my talent.

If these were the only benefits of creativity in my life, it would be enough, but the deepest, most transformative effects of my new commitment go far beyond these. One byproduct of my creative sessions is the addition of times of scheduled solitude into my days. Especially when I write, I need the silence and concentration that solitude offers, and this has given creativity a restorative, spiritually deep quality that I now cannot live without, especially as I'm finding my need for solitude is increasing as I get older. Creativity is meditative, calming me, focusing my attention, and increasing my gratitude for the power of beauty and for the stillness and silence that, for me, enable it. Our world values busyness, action, verbalization, and constant interaction with a network of people and deprecates, by contrast, their counterparts—stillness, silence, and solitude—even making these qualities seem selfish and anti-social. However, our souls need these elements in order to flourish and develop, and ultimately attending to our own growth enables healthier relationships and more productive action. In solitude, I can move at my own pace, choose my own activities, and wrap myself in the silence and relative stillness of time alone. Solitude provides balance to my job as an English professor, where I lead classrooms of students and mingle with colleagues; I truly love my job, so these responsibilities and roles are ones I accept gratefully; yet my natural inclinations nudge me towards solitude, so finding that productive creative work provides more opportunities for solitude is a double blessing.

Of course, if you are more gregarious than I, you can cultivate your social side rather than your solitude through creativity. Studies confirm that creativity can make practitioners feel less isolated and can enlarge their social circle if creativity is practiced in a social setting.[17] There are several ways you can make creativity more intentionally social. For instance, creative time could include a gathering of artsy friends; one of my students at the college where I teach, for example, told me that she has friends who regularly meet at The Bridge, a local coffee shop, to paint together, especially when they need art as stress relief. Taking art lessons or moving your private sessions to public places like coffee shops, parks, or cafes, where conversations would likely pop up or at least you would be stimulated by being near others and their activity, are other options for making creativity compatible with more social impulses.

Whether you use creativity as an opportunity for solitude, as I do, or as a social stimulus, though, both contexts can yield another benefit of creativity, a spirit of giving. This is an aspect of creating that Annie Dillard also celebrates: "One of the few things I know about writing is this: spend it all, shoot it, play it, lose it, all, right away, every time. Do not hoard what seems good for a later place in the book, or for another book; give it, give it all, give it now.... The impulse to keep to yourself what you have learned is not only shameful, it is destructive. Anything you do not give freely and abundantly becomes lost to you. You open your safe and find ashes."[18] As Dillard suggests here, creativity is one way of sharing your interests, your ideas, your viewpoints, your life with others, and research has shown that investing in creativity actually expands a generous mindset, a desire to share with others. When I began my second published book, for example, my main motivation for writing it was because I truly believed that its premise—that combining the benefits of being in nature with the value of

---

17. "5 Big Benefits," paras. 16–19.
18. Dillard, *Writing Life*, 78–79.

Christian meditation—was a God-intended practice that could enrich the spiritual lives of those who engaged in it. I wanted to share that message more widely, which a published book would enable me to do. Making a profit on the book was never my goal, so since its publication, I have either given the book away or sold it at my cost to as many who wanted it. Also, as I started improving in my calligraphy skills, I began to "mass produce" some hand-lettered quotations and phrases onto old dictionary pages. Some of these became "prizes" to the students who weekly had the best thoughts on my class discussion boards, Christmas gifts for family and friends, or "thank you" gifts for the women in my Bible study.

Similarly, my mother took cake-decorating classes just because the skill looked intriguing, but over the years, she baked and decorated dozens of cakes for others, several of which were wedding cakes, for all three of us girls as well as for some church friends. I don't think she charged for any of them. Similarly, my sister Beth shared her gift of piano playing by giving lessons when she was younger and playing for churches she attended as a young adult, and my other sister Teresa, an LPN, is always willing to give medical advice when we come to her with symptoms. These examples of generosity all express gratitude to God for the different creative bents with which he blessed each of us. James Clear acknowledges this same lovely reciprocity of creativity when he points out the fact that art can not only foster a generous mindset, but that the act of giving can itself become a work of art. "As long as you contribute rather than consume, anything you do can be a work of art."[19]

In the previous chapter, I identified imagination and originality as personal characteristics that are conducive to creativity. In a sense, these traits are so intimately connected with creativity that they nearly become a definition of it. I question, in fact, whether it is possible to be creative without imagination and innovation being elements of that process. Their necessity to creativity ensures that they are also valued benefits of any creative practice. As the article "The Significant Benefits of Creativity in the Classroom" points out, creativity fuels all improvements and innovations.[20] Because of this connection, it also seems an obvious truth that consistent dedication to creative expression would always enlarge our capacity for imagination and innovation. Madeleine L'Engle places extreme value upon this imaginative power of creativity, claiming that it not only restores our

19. Clear, "Make More Art," para. 18.
20. TeachThought Staff, "Significant Benefits," para. 19.

once vibrant childhood artistic potential, but also opens us to other worlds that are replete with spiritual possibility: "In art, we are once again able to do all the things we have forgotten, we are able to walk on water, we speak to the angels who call us, we move, unfettered, among the stars."[21]

Although I can't claim to have received such lovely, poetic access to angels or to stars, I can confirm that creativity can lead to greater imaginative capacity and heightened innovation. As I noted in chapter 3, though I began altered books using ideas I had gathered from other artists, as I progressed, I began to form original ideas as well; similarly, studying different styles of calligraphy enabled me to alter the forms of some letters and uniquely design others to fashion my own composite style. In addition, though I used to find it difficult to come up with topics to write about, now it seems that every piece I work on prompts new ideas that lead to my next project. Such was the case with this book, for example. As I was writing my Christian nature meditation book, I became intrigued by the power that meditation and exposure to nature had to intensify creativity, and my curiosity to learn more about creativity was the impetus for writing this book.

As imagination develops and innovation increases, they become more natural facets of the creative work, no longer self-consciously pursued as much as they are a normal, intrinsic part of creation. Our growing confidence and lower self-inhibition introduce new freedom and ease to the process, as does our recognition that there are no necessary rules to follow in creativity.

I have seen this evidenced in my daughter Faith. Though she has always been interested in artistic pursuits, as I have observed her over the years, I have not only seen her skills improve tremendously, but the development of her imagination and originality have especially been exciting to see. As an elementary teacher and a doting aunt to her twin sister's two boys, these two groups are the recipients of most of her creativity. For every birthday the boys have, she designs a T-shirt for them that features their age and emphasizes a particular interest they have at the time. When the Ts accumulate, she plans to make them into quilts that will become records of their younger years, a useful scrapbook of their lives. Similarly, every year she chooses a theme for her classroom and decorates the room and the students' name tags and homework baskets accordingly; she even extends the theme into some of the classroom activities and learning exercises. One year, for example, her treehouse theme involved buying a loft,

21. L'Engle, *Walking on Water,* 57.

bolting small, fallen tree branches from our woods to each corner, creating a canopy over the reading loft with large leaf-shaped fronds, and constructing a translucent "house" on one side of the loft out of visqueen and sticks. She used twigs to spell out inspirational words across the top edge of her wall, adapted *Magic Tree House* episodes as learning modules, and awarded time to read in the loft as rewards for good behavior.

Edgar Degas defined art as "not what you see, but what you make others see."[22] I discovered, though, that practicing creativity also has a profound impact on how I *myself* see and how deeply I notice the world around me. As my discussion in chapter 3 of the importance of attentiveness to creativity has already established, committing to creativity has refined my attentiveness, not only while actively creating, but in all areas of my life. I now look at the world with eyes that are more trained to really see it, not only because everything now is a potential subject for my art, but because the concentration I give to my art has honed my entire range of perception, making me more attentive to detail and nuances of shape, shade, and form, and has heightened my sensory awareness, helping me go beyond a default, automatic dependence on sight to deliberately engage my other senses more fully. In a quote attributed to Orson Scott Card, such attentiveness is a characteristic that deepens over time, providing a steady stream of inspiration for our work. "Everybody walks past a thousand story ideas every day. The good writers are the ones who see five or six of them. Most people don't see any."

I am trying very hard not to be part of the latter group. To fail to attend, to allow myself to be distracted and thus, for all intents and purposes, to be blind to my surroundings dishonors God's creativity through the ingratitude it conveys. A parallel example might help to clarify this point. For several years, I led a college level academic trip to England. One of my biggest frustrations was when I would take the group to the National Gallery or to the British Museum and, because of time limitations, could only give them two or three hours to explore the places on their own. Having not had the opportunity to travel internationally prior to my leading the trip, the richness of what these places had to offer overwhelmed me. I therefore returned again and again to them in my free time. Many of my students, however, seemed disaffected by the treasures these places offered; almost without exception, after the time allotted for exploring these museums was over, I would return to the group and find them sprawled

---

22. Connolly, "Art Is Not."

in the foyer, looking at their phones, where, I discovered later, they had been for over an hour, waiting for me to return. As Christians, we need to guard ourselves against apathy and jadedness, for these attitudes could result in disregard and ingratitude for the gifts of God. Such an attitude could be responsible for the mindset that characterized some in Christ's audience: those who were "ever seeing but never perceiving" and "ever hearing but never understanding" (Mark 4:12). Seeing and hearing are biological capacities, but intentional, persistent alertness yields perception and understanding, both of which suggest the ability to see beyond the material surface of things to access their meaning and significance, a topic I will cover at greater length in the following chapter.

Deep attentiveness not only is an expression of our gratitude to God, but it also expands and deepens our appreciation for beauty, both in others' creative output and in the much wider range of God's creativity evident in nature. Attention to beauty also enlarges our own capacity to create the beautiful and, reciprocally, creating beauty ourselves makes us more attuned to the beauty outside of our immediate creative space. In my life, this reciprocity is most apparent in the interaction that exists between the beauty I observe in nature and its effect upon my writing life. If, for example, I take a solitary walk on a state park trail, almost invariably I find myself constructing sentences in my head that attempt to describe the beauty that I see. I process nearly everything I see through this mental language; walks become drafts. I have difficulty separating my writing craft from the beauty I see or read about, nor do I wish to separate them, for they enrich each other through their interplay. To me, this is one of the most wonderful benefits creativity has to offer, opening our eyes to the presence of beauty in the world, making us more aware and appreciative of the aesthetic components of our lives. Joel Clarkson agrees, claiming that because we ourselves are the handiwork of God (or his poetry, as I earlier noted), we are better enabled to see the poetry in creation. "Hidden within the act of creativity is a unique revelation of the world as it truly is: a poem, a song, a work of art in itself."[23] Michael Card also affirms the intrinsic connection between the beauty of nature and the beauty of God, asserting that the beauty of creation draws us because it reveals the beauty of God.[24] Our attentiveness to nature and our almost instinctual attraction to it are evidences of our need for God; our natural response to the beauty of creation is a desire to create

---

23. Clarkson, "How Creativity Connects Us," para. 5.
24. Card, *Scribbling in the Sand*, 32.

beauty ourselves.[25] A wonderful, seamless Mobius loop of reciprocal and complementary benefit is thus constructed in the interplay between creativity and attentiveness: creativity increases our attentiveness, and heightened attentiveness improves our art; attention to beauty expresses our gratitude to God, and our gratitude deepens our appreciation for beauty; our deeper appreciation for beauty increases our desire to create beauty ourselves; our deepened desire to create beauty results in an increase of our creative activity; increased creativity develops more fully our *imago dei* emulation of God, and increased emulation of God enriches our relationship with him; a deeper relationship with God enlarges our gratitude for the beauty he has imbedded within creation; greater gratitude intensifies our attentiveness to beauty in creation; a greater attentiveness . . .

The interplay of benefits derived from creativity are not limited, of course, to only the benefit of increased attentiveness. All the benefits of creativity demonstrate this reciprocity and complementariness. For example, the increased cognition that creativity enables contributes to the more effective problem-solving ability that creativity also fosters. The stress relief creativity offers would certainly contribute to creativity's mood bolstering effects. The fact that creativity increases focus enables attentiveness to be sharpened and makes our solitude more productive; solitude contributes to lower stress levels, and so on. The number of benefits that we can attribute to creativity are so numerous, in fact, that listing them begins to sound like a late-night infomercial for some overhyped diet aid: creativity has so many and varied far-reaching benefits that it begins to sound too good to be true. But in this case, it is both good and true, because creativity is God-designed, a rich, life-enhancing practice that increases our own joy and satisfaction at the same time that it offers beauty and truth to the world and honors God through the full utilization of our *imago dei* capabilities.

---

25. Card, *Scribbling in the Sand*, 31.

5

A Theology of Creativity

CREATIVITY, AS AN EXPRESSION of *imago dei*, is not frivolous play, a mere diversion, or a casual hobby. It is, as Matt Tommey points out, "a window to the heart of God designed for Him to flow his presence through."[1] Because of this, it has rich spiritual implications, for it is an effort to align ourselves with God, to trace the art of the one who sculpted our own forms and breathed his spirit into us. It makes sense, then, to regard God's—and our—creativity with awe and to consider well its spiritual dimensions by forming a theology of creativity.

The word *theology* means "the study of God," and while creativity is only one small trait of the wholeness of God, it nevertheless is a beautifully deep, vibrant, and infinitely varied attribute that deserves serious thought. Exploring a theology of creativity enables us to practice our creativity with the focus and attitude that is most honoring to God, a commitment that enhances our spiritual lives and even improves the quality of our art through considering creativity's purpose and potential to shape us more fully into God's image.

In considering a theology of creativity, the aptly named critic Art Lindsley argues that we need a "four-chapter gospel" to best understand the role of creativity in our lives. A four-chapter gospel includes an understanding of creation, the fall, redemption, and restoration. As Lindsley explains it, *creation* confirms precisely what I have been presenting as

1. Tommey, *Unlocking the Heart*, Day 6.

truth in this book: that God created all humans with the ability to respond to him, to others, and to creation itself through our own creativity. The *fall*, however, damaged the interrelationship between these elements, tainting not only our relationships with all three but also compromising the beauty and fluidity of our creativity. *Redemption* restored our relationship with God through Christ's intervention for us on the cross, reunited believers in the body of Christ and the Church, and offered the promise of creation's freedom from the curse of sin. Similarly, *restoration* assures us that creation will be remade, not discarded, when Christ ultimately rules in the new heaven and the new earth.

Most Christians, Lindsley claims, focus only on the fall and redemption, the elements that concern our personal salvation, but incorporating creation and restoration into the gospel clarifies our role as Christians in *participating* in the world, not simply seeing ourselves as saved and waiting for Christ's return.[2] Such a view clarifies our responsibility to use our creative capacities to collaborate with God in bringing about restoration through engagement with the world, creating alongside God, and revealing beauty, truth, and meaning through exercising our creative gifts. This perspective provides a firm foundation for a theology of creation.

Alongside this more expansive corporate/communal view of creativity, I would like to suggest a complementary model, one which expresses a more personal and individualistic conception of creativity. This way of thinking about creativity has not only helped me better understand the elements of creativity and how they interact in process, but it has also given me a small bit of insight into that most mysterious of concepts, the Trinity.

Though most of us probably think of the Genesis creation as an act of God working as a single entity, a closer look at the language reveals the Trinity performing in seamless harmony. Genesis 1:1, as we well know, declares that "in the beginning, *God* created the heavens and the earth." Alongside him, however, appearing in verse two, we see that the "*Spirit* of God was hovering over the waters." Additionally, though we know God could have created the world with a mere gesture or even simply by willing it to happen, he chose instead to *speak* the world into existence, so Christ as the *Word* also participated in the event, a truth confirmed in John 1:1. "And God *said*, 'Let there be light,' and there was light" (1:3). Their perfect collaboration illustrates the interaction of the elements of every creation process: God is the creator: the person who performs the creative act. The Spirit is the inspiration: the

---

2. Lindsley, "Why Your Creativity Matters."

element that prompts or motivates the creative process. Christ is the Word: the materials, abilities, media, or supplies used to construct or accomplish the art. Creativity is only possible when all three of these work in harmony, as they did at the original creation of the world. Together, they provide a model that anyone working on a collective project should seek to emulate. Though united in the effort to complete their work, each person of the Trinity contributed his unique talents to the task.

God the creator is, as we are when we exercise our *imago dei* giftedness, the enactor of creativity. As the original Creator, God was the active agent whose mind conceived the plan and whose hands shaped the work. Because of the mystery that is the Trinity, God the creator contains and *is* the inspiration and the Word and not, as a human creator, merely the recipient or manipulator of these; his creative work had a harmony and a cohesion, a perfect unity of effort that we as humans cannot achieve, though our desire should always be to strive for a "fit" between the inspiration that fuels us, the materials we use, and the elements of our identity that make our creativity unique. As creators, we receive inspiration—ideas, motivation, passion—and use it to enrich and guide our creativity. If we think of inspiration only in the conventional way, as some sort of external, ethereal stimulus, it is obvious that most creative work lacks such prompting. However, if we conceive of it more broadly, it is equally obvious that all of our creative output depends upon inspiration. For inspiration can be accessed in multiple ways: it can, of course, be in the form of a revelation from God, but it can also be gained from nature, conversation, experience, brainstorming or research, personal motivation, dreams, contemplation, or even at times, as it was for me, from frustration. God the creator, of course, had no materials, supplies, or media with which to fashion the world but created even these *ex nihilo*; we as sub-creators take what has already been made and make something new with them.

In Genesis, inspiration is the Holy Spirit, the breath of God as he opens his mouth to speak. The word used to refer to the Holy Spirit in the Bible is the same word—*ruach*—used to refer to physical breath as well as to wind,[3] emphasizing both their pervasiveness and the essential role both have in our existence. The Spirit at creation gave life, energy, and animation to the forms God spoke into being, and this same Spirit breathed life into the initially lifeless form of Adam; that breath filled his lungs, urged his heart into motion, and delivered oxygen to his body for the first time.

---

3. Yancey and Brand, "Breath," 404.

Oxygen is essential for life on earth, but something more is necessary for eternal life, life beyond this world, and this was the Spirit's most mysterious gift—he was the breath that stirred a soul into existence, the feature that set mankind apart from the rest of creation. "The Lord God formed the man from the dust of the ground and breathed into his nostrils the breath of life, and the man became a living being" (Gen 2:7). Centuries later, Jesus transferred this same Spirit from himself to his disciples by breathing on them (John 20:22), and a few months later, in the form of a "mighty rushing wind" (*ruach* again) [Acts 2:2], the Spirit swirled into a larger crowd of Christ's followers, infusing their humanity with spiritual essence, fueling fresh fire in their souls, the overflow erupting in flames above their heads.[4] When we live out our *imago dei* identities as creators, we have access to this same spirit, an in-spirit-ing that freshens our work, giving us new ways to see and opening us to beauty, truth, and meaning. The Spirit is our inspiration, the Spirit within.

Unlike our physical breath, which is an automatic function of our bodies and requires no conscious thought on our parts, however, the intake of Spirit, both in our spiritual lives and in our creative lives, must be intentional and ongoing.[5] Physical breathing consists of intake and outtake, and so it must be with our spiritual existence and our creative practice as well. We draw in Spirit and we are *in*spired; if we expel Spirit, we *ex*pire—die. In our spiritual lives, if we do not make a conscious effort to nurture the indwelling of God's spirit within us, our relationship with God will atrophy, and our distance from God may make it impossible for his breath to inspirit us. Likewise, if we are not receptive to the inspirations that surround us, if we do not yearn for the order, beauty, meaning, and transcendence that creativity offers or lack the impulse to worship God, our creative potential will wither. To allow our creativity to lie dormant or become stagnant is to miss out on the rich stimulation of mind and soul that are available to us through nurturing our artistic potential. God intended for our creative work to enhance and deepen our spiritual lives, for "our making is an outward expression of the internal work of God's life-giving breath in us."[6]

The final member of the Trinity, active in Genesis creation and just as vibrantly present today, is Christ the Word. John, through borrowing the syntax of the Genesis account, makes explicit that Jesus eternally coexisted

---

4. Yancey and Brand, "Breath," 406–7.
5. Yancey and Brand, "Breath," 401.
6. Shaffer, "Creative's Role," para. 9.

with God and that he participated fully in creation: "In the beginning was the Word, and the Word was with God, and the Word was God.... Through him all things were made; without him nothing was made that has been made" (John 1:1–3). Christ spoke the words of creation, the words that sent rays of the Trinity's light into the void, dispelling darkness; the words that rolled back the deep and formed dry land. The Word as Scripture guided, inspired, and awed through the ensuing centuries, and when Christ embodied the Word, the Word altered the world forever.

Because writing is my principal expression of creativity, Christ's designation as *the* Word is especially meaningful to me, confirming that he, too, loves language and endows it with the ability to capture and preserve beauty and meaning. However, in the analogy I am establishing between the Trinity and creative process, any medium, any materials, any creative expression can sub in for language—paint, clay, garden plants, food, a song that soothes a crying child, a meticulously organized closet—any creative act can be a part of this trinitarian interrelationship. A human creator, even when inspired, cannot give form or substance to those ideas without the materials to construct and real-ize the vision; this parallels the point I made at the close of chapter 3, where I argued that creativity only has value if energy and action give reality to creative impulses. Just as the Godhead is inseparable, an irreducible math formula in which $3 = 1$, so also the process of creativity is a beautifully complex interaction between creator, the materials of creation, and the inspiration that initiates and sustains the interplay of these two, enabling the aesthetic compositions, innovative thoughts, and fresh perspectives that have the power to transform the materials of God's *ex nihilo* creation into a unique, personal emulation of God.

Considering creativity within these two frameworks—one that understands creativity within the full scope of the gospel message and another that parallels the individual artistic process with the intimate collaboration of the Trinity in creation—provides a solid foundation for a theology of creativity. From there, the theology broadens and expands into a structure that can explicate what it means to create as a Christian. Examining creativity as God intended it to function presents it in its purest form, as an ideal state—a level of perfection, of course, that our human creativity cannot attain. However, a theology of creativity can do no less than to examine it in its pure form. As an ideal, it is a model for us to strive for, providing correctives to our failures and giving us a standard by which to evaluate our own mindsets and purposes. To illustrate how each of these elements influences the practice of creativity in the life of a believer, I have chosen to focus on Flannery O'Connor as an example, for she, as a devout Christian, intentionally and explicitly engaged and modeled a theology of creativity that shaped and defined the literature she wrote.

The fundamental posture that should undergird all of our creativity is submission to God's authority, a position that requires a willingness to surrender our right of absolute creative freedom to God's control. The world—especially the Western world—considers admirable and healthy the traits of independence, autonomy, and self-focus, so submission is for the most part considered a negative impulse. Our society interprets dependency as weakness, autonomy as evidence of maturity, and "self-care" and looking to self-interests before the needs of others as evidence of a healthy identity and a proactive way to protect mental health. The culture of creativity especially privileges these traits through the images of the *avant garde* artist, the Bohemian author, and the brooding musician. In other words, we expect creatives to be radically unique loners living entirely outside of societal expectations, following only the direction of their art. Artists wear berets and paint-daubed smocks and examine the world through a frame they make with their fingers. Writers wear tweedy jackets with leather elbow patches and frequent dim cafes where they scribble in notebooks or hunch over their computers. Musicians hear music in their heads that drowns out the drone of reality; they live in sync with the rhythms of the music only they can hear. Or so we imagine.

To submit, therefore, especially as a creative person, runs counter to these artistic avatars, to society's values, and also to our human instinct to be in control of our lives. We balk at accepting hierarchies and instinctively resist submission in general because it makes us feel vulnerable. We abdicate a portion of our self-governance, freedom, and agency when we submit to someone else's authority, of course, and therefore consider it a position of forfeiture and loss. Submission to God, however, involves a quite different dynamic. Repeatedly the Scriptures urge submission and align it only with benefit: Job 22:21, for example, says, "Submit yourselves to God and be at peace with him; in this way prosperity will come to you." In James, he writes, "Submit yourselves, then, to God. Resist the devil and he will flee from you" (4:7). The outcomes of submission to God are radically different from our submission to other humans and human institutions because of God's perfect nature. His goodness and love assure us that he will always use his fatherly authority to improve us, guiding and correcting us out of his love for us, a love that is never motivated by a power-hungry desire to control or manipulate us. His omnipotence, though a fearful attribute for a human to possess, is, in God's hands, confirmation of his authority over the universe and his unlimited ability to protect us from harm. *Every* attribute of God—his holiness, justice, patience, constancy, omniscience, and grace, to name only a few—should assure us that when we submit our creative freedom to the Lordship of Christ, we can unreservedly trust that our art will not be stymied or restricted in any way harmful to us, but rather that it will be enhanced through offering it to God. The light imagery Madeleine L'Engle utilizes in the following passage conveys well the beauty of such trusting submission to God: "To be an artist means to approach the light, and that means to let go our control, to allow our whole selves to be placed with absolute faith in that which is greater than we are."[7] As Thomas Terry and Ryan Lister also point out, our creativity actually becomes more powerful—and I would add, more affective and effective—when it is in obedience and submission to God.[8] But of course *obedience* is another posture we humans have difficulty adopting, for it too involves submitting our will to God's. We regard obedience as a stifling of our freedom, but as Terry and Lister also clarify, obedience is not the opposite of freedom, because obedience is a *choice* we make; *captivity* is a more accurate opposite of freedom, for captivity is not a choice, but a forced condition.[9]

Flannery O'Connor established her career upon this principle. Her faith was so integral to who she was and what she did that she could not conceive of it not affecting how and why she wrote. In "Novelist and Believer," a speech she gave at Sweetbriar College, she notes that the conference organizers preferred for the speakers not to align themselves with a specific faith tradition but to think of religion more generically as "an expression of man's ultimate concern." O'Connor declined to comply, explaining that her Christian faith was so formative that "for my part, I shall have to remain well within the Judeo-Christian tradition. I shall have speak, without apology, of the Church, even when the Church is absent; of Christ, even when Christ is not recognized."[10] In a letter to John Lynch, she goes a bit further, suggesting that she submits her writing to God's control, so that "ultimately,

---

7. L'Engle, *Walking on Water*, 191.
8. Terry and Lister, *Images and Idols*, 54.
9. Terry and Lister, *Images and Idols*, 115.
10. O'Connor, "Novelist and Believer," 155.

you write what you can, what God gives you."[11] To the claim that such submission restricts her creative freedom, she notes in another essay that

> the Church, far from restricting the Catholic writer, generally provides him with more advantages than he is willing or able to turn to account, and usually his sorry productions are a result, not of restrictions that the Church has imposed, but of restrictions that he has failed to impose on himself. Freedom is of no use without taste and without the ordinary competence to follow the particular laws of what we have been given to do. If writing is your vocation, then, as a writer, you will seek the will of God first through the laws and limitations of what you are creating; your first concern will be the necessities that present themselves in the work.[12]

Thus, though we may fear that submitting our creativity (and our lives) to Christ's control will strip us of our creative freedom, we can trust both O'Connor's position and Terry and Lister's claim that submission actually *improves* our art. Submission offers boundaries, discipline, guidelines, and standards—all of which actually enable creativity, a concept Yehudi Menuhin, the famed violin virtuoso, accepted in his rhetorical question: "Do we not find freedom along the guiding lines of discipline?"[13] Terry and Lister concur, adding that "everything we cherish and build our hopes on demands these things."[14] Unrestricted freedom, by contrast, can result in complete self-indulgence, a loss of boundaries, and a chaos of directionless experimentation.[15]

If submission and obedience still seem confining and negative to you, try thinking about them in the context of raising a child. Children are born helpless, and if parents were not available to meet their every need, they would not survive. However, good parents know that it would be unhealthy to cultivate and extend such a me-centered attitude. As the children grow and become more aware, good parents know it is their responsibility to teach them that they must adapt to certain expectations and requirements, that they must consider the needs and rights of others, and that they cannot do whatever they want to do when they want to do it. Therefore, they establish rules and guidelines to prod their children in the right direction;

---

11. O'Connor, *Habit of Being*, 115.
12. O'Connor, "Church and the Fiction Writer," 152–53.
13. "Yehudi Menuhin Quotes."
14. Terry and Lister, *Images and Idols*, 116.
15. Terry and Lister, *Images and Idols*, 115.

they give them boundaries so they'll feel safe and loved; they set standards for them to aspire to and discipline them when they do things outside of their expectations. God desires our submission and obedience for the same reasons; his parameters also offer clarity, alleviate stress, give useful direction, and provide a sense of safety, contentment, and trust. If we are willing to pursue our talents and express our creativity with God's will preeminent to ours; if we downplay our egos and release our need for personal recognition, desiring instead to promote God through our creativity, we can establish a practice that isn't so full of our own self-interest that it allows no space for God's presence.[16] Only when we submit to God's greater creativity can our own creativity have room to grow.

This level of submission to God of ourselves and of our work, especially a submission that is unreserved, freely given, and trusting, is only possible if we fully embrace humility as the mindset we bring to our craft. As is true of submission, society also undervalues humility. We idolize individual talent, rewarding it with money, fame, fan clubs, media attention, good grades, paparazzi, awards, publication, and adulation. As Bret Lott astutely notes, in our world,

> art for God's sake no longer matters: man, as he has been doing since the garden . . . placed himself on the throne of meaning and purpose; and art, man's creation, intended to be produced in harmony with God, wandered away. The result . . . is an utter preoccupation with the self; the result is an unmoored harmonic line, consumed with believing itself the melody.[17]

Most of us, I think, if we were honest, would admit that at the least we appreciate attention and praise, and we probably wouldn't turn down monetary benefits or fame if either were offered. Even I, remember, in my humble childhood dream of being a writer, wanted to be semi-famous! Recognition, praise, and appreciation for our creativity are not, of course, intrinsically evil, but they should not be the main motives for our work. Michael Card explains well the balance we should work to achieve when he writes that, as Christian creators, our art should be motivated by servanthood, obedience, and humility;[18] such humility keeps the focus off ourselves, our abilities, and our preoccupation with what others think, and onto God.[19] Here again,

---

16. Card, *Scribbling in the Sand*, 80.
17. Lott, "Artist and the City," 39.
18. Card, *Scribbling in the Sand*, 59.
19. Card, *Scribbling in the Sand*, 78.

L'Engle's etymological reminder to us of our earthy origins should keep us humble: "the root word of *humility* is *humus*, earth; to be *human*, too, comes from the same word."[20] This derivation should not make us feel like dirt, however, for God does not want us to be self-deprecating, an attitude that undermines the gifts God has given us.[21] Instead, L'Engle's metaphor should remind us that we are artwork formed in the sculptor's hands.

Ideally, healthy humility is "believing that the giftedness we may indeed possess is not of our own making, that the purpose of its being given is not that we might gain attention and praise for ourselves, but that we might respond in gratitude with our best creative effort to win praise for the One who first gave the gift."[22] Bruce Lockerbie concurs, noting that Christians should view creativity as an offering of thanks to the Creator-God instead of an opportunity to revel in their own role as creator.[23] The real danger in fixating on ourselves is that it makes creativity an idol that we worship[24] instead of directing our worship towards God, the source of our creativity.[25] I like how Harold Best expresses the concept of human deference before God. As he puts it, "no human effort, no matter how noble or magnificent, should ever be capitalized."[26]

Despite her success as a writer, O'Connor certainly did not capitalize her own accomplishments; instead, O'Connor's recognition of her talent as a gift from God fostered a healthy self-deference in her. Writing at a time when there was a surge of creativity in the South, O'Connor regarded herself humbly as a lesser talent among such writers as Tennessee Williams, Eudora Welty, Katherine Anne Porter, Robert Penn Warren, and especially William Faulkner. With her characteristic humor, O'Connor deferred to Faulkner's greater talent, saying that "The presence alone of Faulkner in our midst makes a great difference in what the writer can and cannot permit himself to do. Nobody wants his mule and wagon stalled on the same track the Dixie Limited is roaring down."[27] In contrast to the forceful trajectory and runaway success that O'Connor presents Faulkner

20. L'Engle, *Walking on Water*, 73.
21. Card, *Scribbling in the Sand*, 78.
22. Card, *Scribbling in the Sand*, 79.
23. Lockerbie, *Timeless Moment*, 23.
24. Terry and Lister, *Images and Idols*, 78.
25. Brown, "Series Introduction."
26. Quoted in Card, *Scribbling in the Sand*, 79.
27. O'Connor, "Some Aspects," 45.

as attaining, O'Connor sometimes portrayed herself as a writer bereft of her own talent, but only a humble conduit through whom God formed the work; rather than controlling the work, she allowed the work to lead her, willing to learn from the process: "I write because I don't know what I think until I read what I say."[28] Her statement bears a similarity to Vincent Van Gogh's equally humble comment that "I am always doing what I cannot do yet, in order to learn how to do it."

Another evidence of O'Connor's humility is found in some of her semi-autobiographical characters, perhaps most explicitly in the lead character of "Good Country People," Joy-Hulga Hopewell. Hulga mirrors O'Connor in several ways: she also is an educated, single adult who, as a result of a debilitating condition, returns home to live with an opinionated single mother who, despite her love for her daughter does not understand her or her talent at all. Rather than portraying Hulga more sympathetically, though, as the undeserving victim of circumstances, O'Connor is unreserved in pointing out Hulga's resentment and intentionally irascible personality, as well as her deliberate choices to make herself plain and more annoying. These literary choices for a somewhat autobiographical character convey O'Connor's ability to see her own flaws and own them. Writing to "A," O'Connor comments on a character from another of her stories, "Revelation," who is depicted with the same self-deprecating honesty. O'Connor writes, "Maryat's niece asked her why I had made Mary Grace so ugly. 'Because Flannery loves her,' said Maryat. Very perceptive girl."[29] In this respect, she is perhaps paralleling the humility and acknowledgement of flawed human character that Rembrandt also draws attention to when he painted himself, wearing contemporary clothing, into the crowd scene of *The Raising of the Cross*, an artistic decision that suggests his recognition in himself of a fallenness that makes him complicit in the death of Christ.[30]

Submitting to God and maintaining an attitude of humility can enable us to keep a proper Christian perspective towards ourselves as creators and towards the art we create. Our creativity can only honor God if our intention in producing art is primarily to draw attention to him rather than to ourselves. Brown even suggests that we should change the way we refer to ourselves as artists in order to prioritize our relationship with Christ over our identity as a creator. Thus, instead of calling ourselves Christian

28. Hickey, "What I Learned," para. 2.
29. O'Connor, *Habit of Being*, 579.
30. "Rembrandt Harmensz Van Rijn," para. 7.

artists, Brown suggests that we refer to ourselves as artist Christians, a title that foregrounds our identity in Christ and makes *artist* only an adjective, a modifier of our more essential identity.[31] Shawna Scafe summarizes well the ideas I have presented here and suggests the ideal posture we should take towards our creativity: "[Creativity is] an act of gratitude and worship. We should pursue 'creating' because it is a gift we are given from the Creator. We must do it in reverence to the one who made us, rather than with reverence to all that we can make."[32]

Submission and obedience to God and the humility that enable them together constitute the foundational mindset that we as artist Christians should have towards our creativity, and they also establish the base for a theology of creativity to be built upon. In addition to identifying necessary mindsets, a theology of creativity should also address the purposes of creativity for a Christian. Our overarching purpose, of course, should be to honor God through our creativity, but honoring God has many specific facets and aspects. One specific way to honor God is to create order from chaos, for in doing so, we emulate God's first recorded creative act. At creation, God transformed darkness and void into light and fullness, a perfect and complete creation. The introduction of sin into the world started the unraveling of the seamless fabric God wove, however, so we as Christians should work to repair the fray. Our own creativity can be a stay against atrophy and loss, a persistent reclamation of and investment in God's original order and design. "Art redeems an existence that seems chaotic, formless, even evil. It preserves elements that we see as important, that tell the truth about something."[33] In every creative act, therefore, the artist faces the same task, though in miniature, that God confronted at creation. We begin with only an idea, or perhaps not even that, the materials that we will work with at the onset only a disordered collection of possible tools. We begin, perhaps haltingly, unsure of our direction, lacking confidence in our skills. We sometimes fail, make mistakes, and must begin again. The end product, despite our hopes and efforts, rarely measures up to the vision we have of the art, yet through the process, the undefined has taken shape; the tangle of ideas and materials that we began with have coalesced into a work that has some structure, beauty, and meaning. Annie Dillard metaphorically parallels this process to the building of a house, a house that above all else must be

31. Brown, "Series Introduction," para. 10.
32. Scafe, "Christian Women," para. 8.
33. Lockerbie, *Timeless Moment*, 18.

soundly constructed. "The line of words is a hammer. You hammer against the walls of your house. You tap the walls, lightly, everywhere. After giving many years' attention to these things, you know what to listen for. Some of the walls are bearing walls; they have to stay, or everything will fall down. Other walls can go with impunity; you can hear the difference. Unfortunately, it is often a bearing wall that has to go. It cannot be helped. There is only one solution, which appalls you, but there it is. Knock it out. Duck."[34] Yehudi Menuhin is even more explicit about his deliberate effort to use the elements of music to create "order out of chaos: for rhythm imposes unanimity upon the divergent, melody imposes continuity upon the disjointed, and harmony imposes compatibility upon the incongruous."[35]

No matter what directions my creativity takes—writing, drawing or watercolor, calligraphy, altered books, building, crafting—creating order from chaos is always part of my process and a deliberate motive that urges me forward as well. I may begin a book or an article with only one general idea; I research multiple sources and think about the topic and then must organize my scattered thoughts into a rough outline. I have to cull the related material and discard tangential information, draft and revise, until I have created an order and a focus that move it from disorder into a solid, well-crafted piece. With my altered books, I may begin with a quotation I want to illustrate, then rifle through my supplies to find elements—papers, tags, ribbon, washi tape, collage, stickers, stencils—that would thematically align with the quotation and work together to create an aesthetically pleasing piece. And, especially if we think of creativity's parameters going well beyond the artistic realm, most of us could acknowledge that this purpose governs most areas of our lives. In my teaching, for example, my guiding purpose is often to move students from a state of confusion and disorder to one of understanding and clarity. Even more directly, in my literature classes, as we work towards interpretation of the texts, our goal is to examine the different elements of a story or poem—its word choices, imagery, literary techniques, form, etc.—that at first may seem disparate and unconnected words and ideas and look for patterns and connections that help us make sense of them, with the goal of fitting all the pieces together to form a unified interpretation of the text. If you were to think through your day, I'm sure you'd be able to identify several regular activities in which this purpose, of transforming chaos into form, meaning, and even beauty, is

34. Dillard, *Writing Life*, 4.
35. "Quotes of Famous People."

the driving force: reading the Bible, instructing your children, straightening the house, following a recipe, driving to unfamiliar locations, weeding the garden, praying through difficult situations—even looking through the contents of the refrigerator to determine what you can make for dinner all involve this purpose at least in some degree. Every day, we push against the second law of thermodynamics, the impulse that moves everything in the universe from order to disorder, seeking to slow the process, reverse it, working to restore creation to the beautiful, harmonic state God designed it to have. God especially imbedded this impulse within our creative urge so that the reclamation of beauty, meaning, and order is an intrinsic human instinct that drives us to create and drives us ultimately to him if we follow its natural trajectory. Bruce Lockerbie says, "No work of art exists until its formlessness surrenders to the artist's control, until he takes these scattered elements of thought, idea, intuition, or emotion and embodies these in oils or tones or words . . . This is what we mean when we declare that all art is incarnational, an attempt—however abstract or fluid it may appear—to give flesh and form to an ideal."[36]

Without question or exception, O'Connor's short stories and novels, in both their characters and plots, demonstrate a deliberate movement from chaos to order, almost always effected by the principal character being offered an opportunity of grace through an epiphany, which I will discuss more completely later. To use just one example from the many available in O'Connor's fiction, Mrs. May of "Greenleaf" is introduced as a single mother of two adult boys, frustrated by her sons' lack of ambition and jealous of the prosperity and security that the sons of her hired help are experiencing, despite their lower-class upbringing. Mrs. May's contentment and sense of superiority are thrown into turmoil by what she perceives as the unfairness of the Greenleaf boys' success, an injustice she tries to correct by nagging her boys, criticizing the Greenleafs, and exerting her authority as landlord over the Greenleafs. The story moves from chaos to order, ironically, in a scene in which Mrs. May is fatally gored by the Greenleafs' wayward bull: only at her moment of death can she clearly recognize that her own wrong attitudes towards the Greenleafs—jealousy, arrogance, and disdain for Mrs. Greenleaf's odd but apparently sincere spiritual fervor—are responsible for the chaos she feels. The goring is presented as a sort of twisted love scene in which she is embraced by the bull ("one of his horns sank until it pierced her heart and the other curved around her side and held her in an unbreakable

---

36. Lockerbie, *Timeless Moment*, 17.

grip"), symbolically uniting her with the Greenleafs, a surrender of self that offers her corrective insight and a chance for her own spiritual restoration: "She had the look of a person whose sight has been suddenly restored but who finds the light unbearable."[37] Though consistently severe in the methods by which her characters achieve order, resolution, and insight, the pattern is nevertheless blatant and foregrounded.

Another beautiful, revelatory purpose of creativity—perhaps a purpose that only creativity can accomplish—is to make visible the invisible or the transcendent. As humans, our senses can perceive only the tangible, visible, created world. As Christians, however, we know that there is a world and a reality beyond this—a realm where God resides, a place where our souls will exist forever, but a place our physical senses cannot yet perceive. Only our imagination can conceive of this reality; sensually and cognitively it is beyond our range.[38] That realm can only be known and experienced—at least while we remain in this world—with our imaginations; thus, the only way to access and describe it is through our creative efforts. "We are called to bring the invisible, intangible qualities of the kingdom into the visible world. We are called to purposefully create by the divine Spirit of God."[39] Matt Tommey argues that "to sense what's going on in the Spirit realm through our natural and spiritual senses and translate that reality—the Kingdom—into the earth realm" should, in fact, be the central purpose of our creativity,[40] a view I share: as Christians, God calls us to do this, and as humans, we are compelled to do this for several reasons. One fundamental reason is because God created human beings to be drawn towards the eternal, yet to exist only within the temporal and tangible. Ecclesiastes 3:11 explains the potential conundrum: "he has also set eternity in the human heart; yet no one can fathom what God has done from beginning to end." God did not leave humanity in hopeless and agonized alienation from their desire for the eternal, however; instead, he endowed the material world with beauty and meaning, qualities that provide empirical evidence of his *own* reality, as Rom 1:20 makes explicit: "For since the creation of the world, God's invisible qualities—his eternal power and divine nature—have been clearly seen, being understood from what has been made, so that people are without excuse." As creators

37. O'Connor, *Complete Stories*, 333.
38. Terry and Lister, *Images and Idols*, 60.
39. Shaffer, "Creative's Role," para. 1.
40. Tommey, *Unlocking the Heart*, Day 7.

A THEOLOGY OF CREATIVITY

ourselves, we should have the same desire, to make incarnate through our art the reality of the intangible, for incarnation—meaning that is grounded in the senses, given form we can identify with—is an especially crucial aid to humans in understanding and recognizing meaning.[41]

Likewise, in further emulation of God, our artistic efforts to reveal the transcendent should take multiple forms and be insistent and clear, motivated by the same urge that compelled God: to enable human access to spiritual reality. For at multiple points throughout Scripture, God goes beyond self-revelation through nature to confirm his real presence even more directly and explicitly by embodying himself in perceivable form: to the wandering Israelite exiles, he appeared as a pillar of cloud by day and fire by night (Exod 13:21), and on Sinai he thundered his reality with such awesome loudness that the Israelites begged him to be silent (Exod 20:18–19). So intense was the Israelites' need to "see" God as represented in Moses, in fact, that when he ascended Mount Sinai to receive the Ten Commandments, they were so desperate for a material replacement for God, whom they seem to have regarded as present with Moses on the mountain top but not among them, that they cast an art object, a monstrously misguided act, certainly, but an act that illustrates well the human need for embodied reality.[42] Elijah heard a "still, small voice" (1 Kgs 19:11–13). Belshazzar saw a physical hand composing a dire sentence of death (Dan 5:5). And, of course, the most astounding and significant embodiment of God was Jesus Christ, the incarnation of God himself, God made flesh to dwell among us. Importantly, Christ's designation as Word especially confirms him as the incarnation of meaning because *logos* refers not just to spoken language and its sound, but to the *meaning* it conveys.[43] The huge amount of art throughout the centuries that pictorially depicts God and Christ also evidences the human desire for the incarnate. Thus, creativity's purpose to make visible the invisible meets the human desire, even need, for incarnational reality and gives form and substance to our invisible God through art. As Matt Tommey puts it, "Because the nature of the creative process is prophetically 'gluing together the seen and unseen,' we should always be enlarging and sharpening our unique creative language in order to be able to hear and sense what God is saying, in order to release Spirit-led Kingdom expression in ways that people can understand."[44]

41. Warren, *Annie Dillard*, 105.
42. Shaffer, "Creative's Role," para. 6.
43. Warren, *Annie Dillard*, 103.
44. Tommey, *Unlocking the Heart*, Day 7.

This human yearning for a glimpse of the transcendent is, in my opinion, largely responsible for our attraction to art, both in our observation and appreciation of it and in our own impulse to create it. For what usually captivates us when we observe art is the sense we get of seeing something in a previously unimagined way, or because in it we experience beauty conveyed in a way we feel incapable of expressing, or because the artist awes us by the originality of his or her technique, imagination, or vision, or because we *get* in our gut the meaning the artist wanted to express through the creation of the art piece. All of these responses connect to our innate desire to experience the transcendent and evidence our cloudy recognition of it.

These are the same impulses that move *us* to create. "The thing you love about your creativity—that glimmer of transcendence that captivates you—is actually a distant reflection of the God of Scripture reflected in your image bearing."[45] Our innate desire to seek this "glimmer of transcendence" is what motivates our creativity and is itself perhaps the primary purpose of creativity. God designed all humans to have this desire embedded within them, though only Christians, those who have chosen to have a deep relationship with their creator God, may fully recognize this. Nonbelievers grope more blindly to satiate a need that they may not recognize as fully but which they sense, nevertheless. A path that moves us towards the ultimate transcendence that is God is to embody in our creativity the glimpses of transcendence that we perceive in our material world, the elements that Paul is referring to in Romans that he claims are evidences of God. "Our creativity can help to make the mundane transcendent and help bring the transcendent near";[46] creativity "[ushers] the transcendent into our ordinary, everyday lives while turning our ordinary, everyday lives into something transcendent."[47]

Michael Card believes that this view is what Jesus was offering to his audience in the episode recorded in John 8:1–11. This is the passage in which the Pharisees bring before Jesus the woman caught in the act of adultery. Rather uncharacteristically, Jesus does not immediately respond to the Pharisees' accusations of the woman or to their defiant demands that he confirm their judgements. Instead, he begins writing in the sand with his finger. Card reads Jesus' gesture here as emblematic of the power of art and its effect, for by pausing to "create" something in the sand, he diverts their

---

45. Terry and Lister, *Images and Idols*, 109.
46. Terry and Lister, *Images and Idols*, 60.
47. Terry and Lister, *Images and Idols*, 61.

attention away from their anger and judgement and gives them a glimpse of another world beyond their own.[48] Card points out that the content or form of creativity is not important, his explanation for why we are not told what Jesus drew or wrote in the sand; only the effect is important, and here Jesus transforms shouting and accusation into a space of silence and reflection that allows the accusers to admit their own sinfulness. Human creativity, Card argues, should strive for the same effect—it "cannot hope to be more, and should not be allowed to be less," Card claims.[49]

Flannery O'Connor's fiction takes up Card's challenge and delivers it with force. As mentioned earlier, most of O'Connor's fiction climaxes at a point of grace being offered to a character, and nearly always the point of change involves violence or even the death of the protagonist. O'Connor was often criticized for the extremity of her stories, but she defended her approach by claiming that her audience, being secular and oblivious to the subtle workings of God, needed something more forceful to shock them out of their complacency. "To the hard of hearing you shout, and for the almost-blind you draw large and startling figures," she wrote.[50] One of her best-known stories, "A Good Man Is Hard to Find," does just this. The story centers on a family traveling from Georgia to Florida for vacation. En route, they roll their car and are stranded on the same road that a murderer, recently escaped from prison, is traveling. Because the grandmother foolishly reveals that she recognizes "The Misfit" from news reels, the criminal summarily kills the family members one by one, until only the grandmother remains. Frantic to save her life, she attempts to gain the Misfit's sympathy by engaging him in conversation. As he tells his story, the grandmother for a split second removes the focus from herself and recognizes the Misfit's own needs. When she sincerely reaches out to him, saying, "Why, you're one of my babies," the Misfit feels so exposed and shocked at her sincerity that he kills her, commenting that "she would have been a good woman . . . if it had been somebody there to shoot her every minute of her life."[51] This is transcendence with a vengeance, God in a lightning bolt, as is true for nearly every O'Connor story, but undeniably the invisible is vividly revealed, the characters are yanked out of their self-absorption into a spiritual realm they didn't know existed, and readers are presented with truths that they

---

48. Card, *Scribbling in the Sand*, 16–17.
49. Card, *Scribbling in the Sand*, 17.
50. O'Connor, "Fiction Writer," 34.
51. O'Connor, *Complete Stories*, 103.

cannot miss. O'Connor's fiction accomplishes the same purpose Yehuda Menuhin claims for music, but with decidedly more dissonance. In a quote attributed to Menuhin, he says, "Music lives and breathes to tell us who we are and what we face. It is a path between ourselves and the infinite."

Another purpose of Christian creativity, closely related to revealing the transcendent, is to convey the meaning intrinsic in the created order. Practicing our own creativity makes us more able to discern that meaning and, even more wonderfully, participate with God to create meaning ourselves. God could have, in theory, created a merely material world—beautiful, functional, but with no intrinsic meaning. Such a world, of course, would have run counter to his plan for humanity from the beginning, for to create humans without a yearning for meaning and purpose would have made them unresponsive to his offer of salvation and relationship with him. L'Engle expresses well the immense value of the world's meaningfulness and accurately identifies its function when she writes that "meaning makes a great many things endurable—perhaps everything."[52]

God established an integral relationship between the created order and meaning in the act of creation itself: he began with *nothing*, or what Genesis can only refer to as chaos and void, and transformed them into order, design, meaning, and significance. It is especially apropos that the first act of creation was the introduction of light into the world, for ever since then, light has served as a symbol of God himself as well as of insight, understanding, and *meaning*, a symbol for the ongoing meaning that exists in creation. In the Gospel of John, John clarifies the depth of this association by using the creation language of Genesis to speak of Christ the Word's role as light in the darkness. In his Gospel, there are twenty-one references to Christ as the light and only seven mentions of darkness in order to make clear the superior force of God and the meaning he gives to creation against the relative weakness of darkness or Satan. Even the fact that John mentions light three times more than darkness may be intentionally significant, indicating the combined power of the trinity against the forces of chaos and void.[53]

Not only does John associate light with Christ the Word, but light also connects with life and truth, other attributes of God, of course, but traits which also align with creativity. The Word is equated with life thirty-five times in John, reiterating God's role as creator, initiating life

52. L'Engle, *Walking on Water*, 56–57.
53. Warren, *Annie Dillard*, 103.

into the world; its association with truth also confirms that the light of the world is "an underived original source, making the incarnate Word the source of any previous illumination or meaning";[54] importantly, all three of the associations that John makes with Christ—the word, life, and truth—suggest that language, life, and truth (and the meaning that each contains) were, like Christ himself, preexistent to humanity's creation, a point I will return to later.

There are, of course, some who believe that there is no meaning in creation; most who hold this opinion are atheists. It makes sense that if God is the source of all meaning, the creator of a meaningful world, that those who reject God's reality would also reject the existence of meaning. I would hold that those remaining who claim to believe that God exists yet do not acknowledge that meaning also exists have not truly been attentive to the world or receptive to God, since attentiveness to both makes obvious the reality of both. As Annie Dillard points out, three stances towards the existence of meaning in the world are possible: the first is to believe that nothing has meaning—people's efforts to argue otherwise are only feeble efforts to create meaning where there is none. A second stance is to believe that meaning exists, but that we have no access to it—our efforts to interpret the world are therefore futile. The third stance, and the one Dillard accepts, is the one the Bible and Christianity also confirm: that meaning exists and that we can know it, at least in part, and contribute to it ourselves.[55]

Because we as Christians align ourselves with this stance, we should approach our creative work with seriousness and purpose that come through in what we produce; what we create should be intrinsically meaningful, worthy of our audience's attention and time. A statement Annie Dillard makes about her own approach to writing is startling in its bluntness, starkly conveying this truth: "Write as if you were dying. At the same time, assume you write for an audience consisting solely of terminal patients. That is, after all, the case. What would you begin writing if you knew you would die soon? What could you say to a dying person that would not enrage by its triviality?"[56] Not surprisingly, when I saw this quoted online in a blog forum, one of the respondents mocked the passage, commenting that "we should put old Annie on suicide watch," missing, or probably more accurately, willfully denying its uncomfortable

---

54. Warren, *Annie Dillard*, 104.
55. Dillard, *Living by Fiction*, 129–30.
56. Dillard, *Writing Life*, 68.

truth; that respondent, lacking any investment in a theology of creativity, saw only morbidity in Dillard's statement rather than its emphasis on purpose, meaning, and transcendence.

What is only a rhetorical question in Dillard's quotation above was a sober reality in O'Connor's life. Knowing that her father had died of lupus, O'Connor was aware that lupus would shorten her life as well; she therefore lived with an immediacy and purpose that gave her writing particular urgency. Because she considered her writing career a God-given vocation, O'Connor believed that the purpose of her art should be to draw people to Christ, to point out to them the spiritual emptiness of their values, and to show them their need for salvation. Because her stories were therefore fraught with spiritual implications and specific meaning, O'Connor was understandably frustrated and sometimes even horrified at some readers' gross misinterpretations. With so much at stake in her intentionality, O'Connor could not bear to expose her stories upon publication to what she regarded as undiscerning readings. For example, in her response to a letter written by a college professor which contained his reading of "A Good Man Is Hard to Find," O'Connor's frustration is clearly evident: "If teachers are in the habit of approaching a story as if it were a research problem for which any answer is believable so long as it is not obvious, then I think students will never learn to enjoy fiction. Too much interpretation is certainly worse than too little, and where feeling for a story is absent, theory will not supply it. My tone is not meant to be obnoxious. I am in a state of shock."[57]

Clearly, not all creators consciously strive to convey meaning through their art, as O'Connor did, nor do I mean to suggest that all creativity must be explicitly religious or evangelistic, even for believers.[58] Nor is there a particular form or style or even a certain level of talent required to express meaning.[59] For example, some of my writing, as is the case with this book and the one that preceded it, openly and unabashedly speak of my relationship with God, and my purpose in writing those books was to draw others closer to God through the practices of meditation and creativity, respectively, but the book that preceded those, while it does discuss how Dillard's faith informs her conception of language, was a book written for a mostly secular academic audience. The things I draw, the content of my altered books, the calligraphy I design, the craft projects I do, and even some of the

57. O'Connor, *Habit of Being*, 437.
58. Card, *Scribbling in the Sand*, 138.
59. DeWeese, "'White Hot Inspiration,'" para. 14.

nature pieces I write more often than not do not explicitly reference God. Yet through all the forms my creativity takes, I am seeking out meaning, exploring its edges, and through my seeking, trying to understand God more fully. For *all* meaning has its origins in God; without God, there is no meaning. C. S. Lewis wrote that "God cannot give us happiness and peace apart from himself because it is not there. There is no such thing."[60] His claim can be expanded to include meaning—there is no such thing as meaning apart from God. Just as God has instilled within every human being's soul a desire for the transcendent and its accompanying desire to make the transcendent incarnate, so does he give all humans a yearning for meaning. These two desires are so connected as to be almost indistinguishable from each other. These desires are most pronounced and explicit in Christians, of course, because through our pursuit of God and choosing a relationship with him, we demonstrate that we have identified the source of meaning and that our desire is to foreground that meaning in our lives. Nonbelievers have the same yearning for meaning but have not yet recognized or acknowledged that its source is in God; therefore, they attempt to discover it in a variety of other misplaced or indirect areas.

As I argued in my previous point, I believe creativity is one of the most productive ways to pursue and express the transcendent, the origin of all meaning, which explains in part why so many are drawn to it. Creativity, which is so personal and varied, provides multiple avenues for exploring and expressing the human urge for meaning. Sometimes art and creativity reflect a misguided search; at other times they reveal true meaning, the meaning found in God, but most serious art, I believe, evidences a search.

Though I do believe that the human urge towards meaning is a frequent motivation for art, I do not believe that all creativity expresses deep meaning, nor is it required to. Sometimes art is merely playful or experimental, both of which, of course, can lead to the discovery of meaning, but sometimes the artist does not pursue it that far. And that's okay. Creativity has value beyond its pursuit or expression of meaning. We may find its value in its innovation, its depiction of beauty, or simply in the joy of process. For example, I love the later paintings of J. W. W. Turner, though they are sometimes impressionistic to the point of obscurity, because of the way his stippled swaths of color beautifully convey light and haze. Similarly, I admire Picasso's *Man with a Clarinet* for the tonality of its muted grays, which I find attractive, and I admire his originality of perspective, the way

---

60. Lewis, *Mere Christianity*, 54.

the painting forces us to see the whole as the sum of its parts. I wouldn't agree, however, that there is any significant message conveyed through either Turner's later work or Picasso's *Man with a Clarinet,* though I do see them as aesthetically pleasing, significant, and thought provoking; their value lies, at least for me, in their innovation and form. Likewise, Ezra Pound's poem "In a Station of the Metro" has no submerged meaning, but there is a stark beauty in its urban scene described through the use of a natural image of blossoms on a black bough, and it allows for meaningful reflection by way of the images it uses.

It should be obvious, however, that I prefer art that embodies meaning and attempts to convey it. I became an English major because I loved literature that required interpretation, writing that had such depth that it was impossible for all of its meaning to lie on the surface. Though some of my students claim to prefer literature that is straightforward and "says what it means" instead of "hiding it," this is the kind of literature I like the least and therefore tend to exclude from my syllabi. I prefer literature that forces me to think, even literature that seems confusing and disordered at first. I love the challenge it offers my students to look for connections and patterns in the text, to trace imagery and analyze word choices, to discover multiple interpretations that a text can contain. I love starting with a text that seems obscure and incomprehensible to my students—or to me!—and through attending closely to its language, form, and style and digging beyond its surface, being able to make sense of the work and discover order, unity, and meaning where they first seemed not to exist. The most rewarding and the most crucial part of my job is helping students refine their attention to detail and develop their ability to discover and comprehend such meaning for themselves.

One of my favorite texts to use to illustrate that meaning and intentionality can exist even in the most seemingly chaotic of contexts is a poem by e. e. cummings called "Bright." On the page, it is literally unreadable—a jumble of words disconnected from context, words with letters randomly capitalized within them, dozens of question marks dotting the page, erratic line and stanza breaks. With promptings, however, students start to discover ways to make sense out of what is seemingly nonsense: they start by recognizing that nearly all the words are adjectives; then they find the only noun in the poem which the adjectives must describe—*star*. They notice that the word *star* gradually appears as letters replace question marks and that the word *bright* suddenly disappears when question marks replace letters. With more guidance, they realize that every adjective appears in the poem as many times as it has letters. Eventually they come to understand that the poem itself—and their gradual progress towards interpreting it!—graphically illustrate the process of creation: moving from a chaotic void to a miraculous order and design.

Their growing interest and engagement as we interpret the poem together further confirms the claim I have been arguing, that God created humans with an innate hunger for meaning, though some squelch, replace, or run from that urge. Both our innate desire for meaning and our need for incarnational representations of it naturally prod us towards meaning-making ourselves. This does not mean that we "make up" meaning for a world in which it is absent, for meaning, since it originates in God, is preexistent to us. Nor am I suggesting that the existence of meaning is contingent on human recognition or response; meaning would exist whether humans noticed or responded to it or not. However, as Dillard points out, God wants meaning to be accessible to humans for their benefit.

> Our human endeavor is to extend the boundaries of sense and meaning; it is to shift phenomena one by one out of the nonsense heap and arrange them in ordered piles about us. If you argue that this endeavor yields only a human kind of sense, and that our interpretations yield only human meanings, not absolute meanings, you will be required to propose a definition of meaning that is not, first and last, meaning for people.[61]

This "endeavor" to explore meaning, to interpret it, to fathom it, and to participate in it by adding to it our own discoveries about meaning and our own efforts to incarnate it is what creativity is all about. Our creative work is driven by our love for beauty, our desire to create order, and our urge to reveal the transcendent, but perhaps our strongest motive in creating is to explore and interpret meaning for ourselves, and through the creation of an art object—or, more broadly, through creatively engaging the world in *any* way—to share our views and vision with others, to invite them to interact with the meanings we offer, and to allow them to discover the meaning they perceive in our work. Dillard beautifully describes creativity's power in the following passage, which applies these points to her chosen field of creativity, writing, though her comments can apply to any creative effort:

> Why are we reading [creating], if not in hope of beauty laid bare, life heightened and its deepest mystery probed? Can the writer isolate and vivify all in experience that most deeply engages our

---

61. Dillard, *Living by Fiction*, 132–33.

intellects and our hearts? ... What do we ever know that is higher than that power which, from time to time, seizes our lives and reveals us startlingly to ourselves as creatures set down here bewildered? ... We still and always want waking."[62]

Practicing creativity inexorably "seizes" us into engagement with meaning. Almost by definition, creativity assumes that meaning exists, for as Dillard reminds us, it "engages our intellects and our hearts" to explore the world at a deeper level, where meaning resides, and in its intended and purest form, it leads us to its source. From that deep well, we receive inspiration to re-create and offer our own expressions of meaning to our audiences. Creativity, in this view, becomes a wonderful collaboration with God, the original and ultimate creator. As Madeleine L'Engle reminds us, "there is something healthily affirming about such structure, a promise that we have a part in the making of meaning. This is not a false promise or an unreal self-control but a promise that we are co-authors with God in the writing of our own story."[63]

Another important element necessary to a theology of creativity is adherence to a moral standard in our art that reflects the holiness of God and which ultimately espouses a redemptive view, informed by our relationship with Christ. Sadly, though Scripture confirms that this is an expectation of us as Christians, its application to Christian creativity is debated and sometimes even eschewed by Christian creatives themselves. A commitment to moral standards in our work of course runs counter to the trends in our society. Quite obviously, we live in a world that has little interest or investment in honoring God, because the majority lack a relationship with God that would steer their work towards this purpose. This is not surprising, but it *is* disturbing, even frightening, according to Madeleine L'Engle: "It is frightening," she writes, "to have to accept the fact that much that has passed for art in this century has depicted distortion, meaninglessness, destructiveness. And it is interesting to note that when the art of the absurd was at its height, theologians began to announce the death of God."[64] In fact, the trajectory of most secular creativity today moves in an antithetical direction to that of Christianity. It is trendy to produce work that is dark and edgy, that questions the existence of meaning, that wallows in hopelessness and accepts despair. Neither is immoral behavior depicted as sinful or soul damaging, but rather as normative and

62. Dillard, *Writing Life*, 72–73.
63. L'Engle, *Walking on Water*, 164.
64. L'Engle, *Walking on Water*, 163.

unchallenged. Again, we should expect such a worldview in those who have not submitted their lives and their art to God. What is particularly disturbing to me, however, is when believers participate in this dark vision and reflect the same worldview as nonbelievers in their own work. They defend it by arguing that it is a realistic depiction of reality, and that it is brave and necessary to face these realities.

It is true, of course, that darkness and struggle are real, and that Christians are not exempt from them, but because of the hope we have through our faith, we should view the world from a different perspective. In order for our creativity to function as worship, it must be in line with the character of God, particularly his holiness. God's creation, the model for our own creativity, was declared good by God himself; our own creativity, an emulation of God's, should also provide the world with something good.[65] As artist Christians, therefore, whom God calls to produce art that honors him and reflects his nature, we should not allow our work to veer without judgement from God's moral standards. Bret Lott offers a lucid and reasoned perspective on this matter. "The created world has a moral order to which we must submit, and through that submission and only that submission will harmony and truth even begin to be approached by us who profess to practice art."[66] Continuing his musical metaphor, Lott alludes to Frances Schaeffer's concept of major and minor themes expressed through creativity and argues that Christian art can represent both, though he nevertheless challenges Christians to ultimately offer a redemptive view of the world, since that is, in fact, the ultimate reality in Christ. God, Lott says, should provide the melodic line, while we as sub-creators should harmonize with him. Because a consistent and stable moral order governs God's melody, if dissonance occurs, it is because the artist's harmonic line has wandered from God's melody.[67]

> Creating in harmony with God does not call for the art to be necessarily upright and pleasing, nor does it call for the artist to be healed and happy. But in this day, when we as believing artists . . . live in a day and age when the artist no longer creates in anonymous humility but has been crowned with many crowns and is not expected to show up on time, and when his art seeks at worst to rub our noses in the stained carpet of his beliefs about us all, and at best seeks to show us the glory we have earned

---

65. Gentry, "Theology of Making," paras. 26–30.
66. Lott, "Artist and the City," 34.
67. Lott, "Artist and the City," 36.

for ourselves, we as believers seeking harmony with God's order must write with a redemptive view of man.[68]

L'Engle is in agreement with Lott when she claims that "there is no subject which should, in itself, be taboo . . . it is *how* it is included which makes its presence permissible or impermissible."[69] For example, the Bible records multiple stories that are dark and disturbing. Some, like the passages found in Ezek 16, are described in graphic detail that is cringe-worthy. Yet never are these depictions of gross sinfulness presented in a manner that condones them or revels in their description. Thomas Howard poses a question that has been a guide for me throughout my teaching career as I make decisions about what works to include in my syllabi; it is a question we should also ask of our own creativity to ensure that what we produce is in keeping with this principle: "Does there come a point at which the artistic portrayal of evil crosses a certain line and itself begins to participate in the very evil it is portraying?"[70] For example, Flannery O'Connor's stories, as should be obvious from the examples I have given in this chapter, could never be accused of excluding the ugliness of sin: rape, murder, lechery, pride, atheism, smug self-sufficiency, and prejudice all appear in her corpus; nevertheless, she insisted that her primary purpose in writing was to convince a secular audience of their need for Christ. "One of the awful things about writing when you are a Christian is that for you the ultimate reality is the Incarnation, the present reality is the Incarnation, and nobody believes in the Incarnation; that is, nobody in your audience. My audience are the people who think God is dead. At least these are the people I am conscious of writing for."[71] Thus, as I stated earlier, her graphically violent stories present an opportunity for grace and an ultimately redemptive worldview. O'Connor offers further perspective on her position, arguing that a Christian writer is obligated to present reality accurately, not avoiding the ugly, while at the same time treating reality with a "prophetic vision" that reveals the "ultimate reality" found in God.

> The Catholic fiction writer is entirely free to observe . . . He feels no need to apologize for the ways of God to man or to avoid looking at the ways of man to God. For him, to "tidy up reality" is certainly to succumb to the sin of pride. Open and free

---

68. Lott, "Artist and the City," 43.
69. L'Engle, *Walking on Water*, 43.
70. Howard, "On Evil in Art," para. 5.
71. O'Connor, *Habit of Being*, 92.

observation is founded on our ultimate faith that the universe is meaningful, as the Church teaches. . . . It is one of the functions of the Church to transmit the prophetic vision that is good for all time, and when the novelist has this as a part of his own vision, he has a powerful extension of sight.[72]

Ultimately, as Christians, our creativity should reflect a redemptive view of the world as well. God calls us to be different and to be difference makers: speaking to his disciples, Jesus addressed the former: "'You are the salt of the earth. But if the salt loses its saltiness, how can it be made salty again?'" (Matt 5:13) He addresses the second purpose in his last prayer before his crucifixion: "'They are not of the world, even as I am not of it. Sanctify them by the truth; your word is truth. As you sent me into the world, I have sent them into the world. For them I sanctify myself, that they too may be truly sanctified'" (John 17:16–19). What we produce by our creativity is "a statement of faith—a profession—that what you have [produced] is good, and worthy, and true."[73] This, of course, is hard, counterculture work, but it is work that is worthy and true, worship in the truest sense of the word. It is a theology worth investing in.

The postures that enable art—humility and submission to God—and the purposes that creativity has—to create order from chaos, to incarnate the transcendent, to convey meaning, and to present a redemptive view of the world—all contribute to and culminate in the ultimate purpose of creativity: to worship God, the originator of all creativity. But, just as we often have too narrow a definition of creativity, so also we may have a too restrictive idea of what constitutes worship. For most Christians, when we think of *worship*, the first image that comes to our minds is a room full of believers led by a praise band lifting their hands towards God. This is, of course, a legitimate form of worship, but worship is severely restricted if we confine it to the boundaries of a church, if we perceive it as only communal, or if we regard it as an "event" separate from our normal routine. Worship should be a mindset, not an activity, that infuses our days, a frame of mind that is as natural as breath. Worship has no time frame or length, no prescribed method, no criteria for success except expressing gratitude and giving honor to God. Worship is lingering over a sunrise, waiting for the vivid strips of orange, lavender, and red to drip into each other, melted by the fierce yellow of the ascending sun. It is gathering shells on a beach or running and being grateful for our body's capabilities—heaving lungs,

72. O'Connor, "Catholic Novelists," 178–80.
73. Lott, "Home," 137.

pounding heart, foot flexion and stretching tendons; cheerfully cleaning up the mess of dropped food under the high chair instead of complaining about it, mowing the grass in careful swaths that overlap just enough to avoid "mowhawking" the yard, skipping lunch so you can prepare a bit better for your next class, or shaping words in your notebook to meditate on a slow saunter you took just before dusk. Any activity you do with an intent of honoring God is sacred, is worship, and that includes creativity. "Every act of creativity, in its essence, is an act of worship, a doxological expression of our true humanity and purpose."[74] One of my students, Kailian Blohm, expressed beautifully the ideal symbiosis that can exist between creativity and worship, writing that

> worship is the foundation and compass by which we create. If God created the celebration of Him through worship and the celebration of His creation through creativity, and if He as a Creator worthy of praise has these united within Him, then it is unreasonable to believe we can divide worship and creation and still do justice to either. It would be creation in a vacuum, cut off from its context, made less than it was meant to be. Worship also directs our creation because it directs us. It points us to the One who made us in His image and guides us back to that image when we're tempted to tie our work to an agenda that leads to inauthenticity and ultimately, a distortion of His image in us.

I worship God in many ways, but I worship most frequently through creativity, because I believe, as Johann Sebastian Bach wrote, that "creativity is a devotional practice, an act of worship." Bach, who signed almost three-fourths of his music with the letters SDG (*soli Deo Gloria*—for God's glory alone) would concur. In his Bible, alongside 2 Chr 5:13, Bach wrote the following: "At a reverent performance of music, God is always at hand with his gracious presence."[75] Of course, not every act of creativity is an act of worship; if we don't approach it with an intention to make the time sacred, entering into it with a mindset that lacks the elements I've described so far in this book—humility, submission, and a desire to discover meaning, order, and the transcendent and to honor God's standards through our work—creativity has little power to draw us to God and to make us more like him. However, "when we approach creativity as a devotional practice, experiencing God's presence is placed at the center of our process."[76] Un-

---

74. Terry and Lister, *Images and Idols*, 13.
75. "Johann Sebastian Bach."
76. Patenaude, "On Becoming Creative," para. 1.

fortunately, even explicitly Christian practices, if entered into thoughtlessly or tainted by pride, can lack a spirit of worship: I have heard many prayers (and, sadly, have offered some myself) that are devoid of anything that would suggest genuine desire to converse with God—they are perfunctory, ritualistic, or prepared to impress an audience rather than to talk to God; I've even heard plagiarized prayers. Similarly, reading the Bible can be just as lifeless if we read it just to meet a chapter quota for a daily goal, or if our mind and our hearts don't engage with what we read. Creativity has *potential* to honor God, to feel his presence, and to solidify our identification with God at the same level that prayer, meditation, Bible reading, or acts of service have, but that potential is only realized when we engage in it with a focus on God—not on ourselves as creators, but upon him as the one we emulate; not with an interest on the excellence of the work as demonstrating our skill but with a desire to do our best work because it fully utilizes our gifts. All worship fails if we enter into it mechanically or ritualistically, or if its focus is not to honor God and to praise God's divine attributes.[77]

In my case, focusing more on my creativity with the goal of not squandering the gifts God has given me and with the intent to produce products that can turn others' attention to God has quite literally transformed my life, as I claimed in chapter 3, adding a dimension to my spiritual life that I didn't really know I was missing until I started investing more time in it. Because I believe my writing can have the most wide-reaching effect on others and because I feel it is my greatest area of giftedness, I have put more time and effort into enlarging that facet of my creativity than other areas. Madeleine L'Engle, in paralleling her writing with prayer and worship, perfectly characterizes my own attitude towards my writing:

> To work on a book is for me very much the same thing as to pray. Both involve discipline. If the artist works only when he feels like it, he's not apt to build up much of a body of work. Inspiration far more often comes during the work than before it, because the largest part of the job of the artist is to listen to the work and to go where it tells him to go. Ultimately, when you are writing, you stop thinking and write what you hear. To pray is to listen also, to move through my own chattering to God to that place where I can be silent and listen to what God may have to say.[78]

Though writing is the form of creativity that most naturally expresses worship in my life, I try to use my other areas of creativity as forms of

---

77. Terry and Lister, *Images and Idols*, 29.
78. L'Engle, *Walking on Water*, 176.

worship and witness as well. I have given my calligraphy quotes—some of which are Christian in focus—to others as a witness. My altered book pages are often outgrowths of my Bible readings or of my time spent meditating in nature, attempts to put into visual form the insights I have gained and the presence of God I have felt when worshipping in those ways. My drawings give detailed attention to the beauty and design of God's creation and increase my awe of his genius. Of course, not all of my creative time is worshipful in nature, but I try to be intentional in focusing some of it in that direction, and when this happens, I can feel the difference in my process and see the difference in my products. When I approach creativity as worship, the time I spend with it feels restorative and unrushed, and my products, whether creative nonfiction, watercolors, or craft projects, often come together more easily. Creativity-as-worship is not a "trick," of course, a way to somehow mystically improve our work, as though in gratitude for our attention, God blesses the time we dedicate to him by intensifying our talent. There is no direct causal relationship between the quality of my work and the degree to which I devote my creativity to God, but my time is more satisfying and restful, as is true of any time I set aside for him.

Developing creativity can sometimes be a difficult task. Living our lives for Christ can be even harder. To be an artist Christian, then, is doubly difficult, because it demands that we be excellent not only in our field of expertise but that we display excellence in how we frame our creativity and how we choose the standards we apply to our creativity to shape it. Again, we can compare how and why we create to raising our children in the faith. We do not train them in the ways of God so that people will admire us as parents for our high standards or for our dedication, nor is our primary motive to increase others' admiration of them. Our motive for the hard work of Christian parenting is to enable them to reflect the nature of God; this is our "living sacrifice," the gift we return to God in gratitude for his initial gift to us in giving us our children. Our creativity is also a gift from God. If we use it only to bring attention to ourselves or only to awe people by our skill or technique, we are misusing the gift. God shares his creative nature with us to enable us to be more like him, to reflect his beauty, to comprehend his meaning, and to reveal his transcendence. Anything less is merely human, not divine.

6

Establishing a Practice and Place

- "I know I should exercise more often—but my schedule is already too packed."
- "I would like to give Christmas gifts that I've made myself, but the holidays are just so busy."
- "I wish I could spend as much time as you do being creative, but I just don't have the time."

I HAVE HEARD COMMENTS like these from probably hundreds of people over the years—at times, I've heard myself claiming the same. It's not surprising that lack of time is the number one excuse given, as it was with me, for not practicing creativity—or accomplishing anything, for that matter. But it is less about *having* time and more about *making* time for what matters. Nora Roberts is credited with saying, "A writer never finds the time to write. A writer makes it. If you don't have the drive, the discipline, and the desire, then you can have all the talent in the world, and you aren't going to finish a book." I didn't suddenly have big blocks of time open up in my schedule to make creativity happen when I made my resolution to create; instead, I reprioritized my time, determining that I would not let less important things eat up the time I could be using to be creative. Think about the time we waste daily on foolish or unnecessary activities: for example, women spend 136 days of their lives "getting ready" (putting on makeup, dressing, grooming), and Americans waste a full five years surfing the internet.[1] Watching TV is the biggest American time suck, consuming 2.8 hours of our time daily.[2] I vowed to use my time pursuing the things most important to me, believing Thoreau's claim that we "cannot kill time without injuring eternity."[3]

If you consider yourself too busy to regularly practice creativity despite your desire to do so, give yourself this challenge: for one week, keep as accurate of a record as you can of what you do in your free time (any time you're not working, sleeping, or eating) and how much time you give to these activities. After a week, add up the minutes to get a total. Most people are shocked by how much "free" time they fritter away or how much time they waste in activities that aren't important to them. Of course, you use some of your leisure time for pursuits that you value—like spending time with children or grandchildren, reading a good book, or even straightening the house. But you will also undoubtedly find that you've spent a good deal of time with mindless, unproductive "filler" activities, like playing video games, surfing the web, watching TV, playing solitaire on your phone app, or dismantling the dryer exhaust looking for lost socks. Repurpose this wasted time and invest it in creative activities, and I can guarantee that you will feel more productive, that you'll have more energy and happiness, and that your creativity will improve exponentially.

It is also helpful to remember that we can tuck creativity into moments. I used to think that if I didn't have a block of time long enough to make substantial progress on a project that it wasn't worth even beginning. This attitude, however, made every artistic project feel like a huge job with an end point nowhere in sight rather than a multiphased, incremental journey with many fascinating and surprising paths, which is how I now view creativity. I may only have time to research one fact I want to add to a piece in progress, or I may only gesso a few pages in different altered books I'm working on instead of launching into the more involved work of mapping out a new page. Kate Mosse explains the benefit of approaching artistic practice in this way:

> Five minutes of writing a day is better than no minutes. Too many new writers think that unless they have plenty of time, it's not worth booting up the computer or sharpening that pencil. But think of it, instead, like practicing scales on the piano before

1. "30 Surprising Facts."
2. Bureau of Labor Statistics, "Time Spent," para. 3.
3. Thoreau, *Walden*, 4.

tackling that Beethoven Concerto or like warming-up [sic] in the gym—the more you prepare for writing, the better shape you'll be in once you have time to really concentrate.[4]

Studies have shown that it realistically takes between eighteen and 254 days to form a habit. That wide span probably accounts for the radical differences in the personalities and motivation that any given group of people possesses, from quick adapters to more laid back, gradual types. Using these numbers for an average, however, suggests that it takes about sixty-six days to transform a new activity into automatic, natural behavior. My creativity practice has well exceeded that length of time, and now I don't have to be intentional about incorporating creativity into my day; it now is so integral to what I do that if for some reason I have to forego it, I sense its absence as a loss in my day.

What element aids this transition into habit most effectively? Consistency. Consistency is the number-one determinant of whether an activity becomes a habit, more important than the quality of your session or the amount of time you devote to your work or the level of challenge that the work presents to you. In fact, these expectations might actually dissuade you, at least at first, from consistency by making you feel you have to dedicate a certain set amount of time to creativity, or that the block of time you have has to be supercharged and efficient, or that you have to produce amazing work every session. I'd suggest you ignore every inspirational poster that you've ever seen with its lofty, idealistic sentiments and instead aim low. Don't expect much of yourself. Give it your some. That way, if you fail to meet your expectations, as is inevitable for all of us at times, you will not get discouraged and give up before you really get started.

Once it becomes a habit, I can assure you that the amount of time you spend in creative pursuits and the quality of your work will both increase, but only consistent practice will get you to that point. When I began to run for exercise, I put very little emphasis on the quality of my workouts because for me, a slow-twitch plodder, there wasn't any quality to be had! I did not work on increasing my speed, nor did I push myself to hit my cardiovascular limits. Neither did I demand of myself any minimum time frame or mileage goal for each workout. I just showed up and committed to running, however fast or far or slow or short my run might be for that day. The same principle works in establishing a practice of creativity.

---

4. "Interview with Kate Mosse," para. 16.

So at first, commit only to consistency—to doing something creative daily, as I did. Give yourself permission to define very broadly what creativity means, so that if time is short on any given day, or if you don't feel particularly motivated, you can still meet your goal of giving some amount of attention to some sort of creative activity. In my case, to become more dedicated as a writer was my most desired outcome in vowing to create daily, yet when I first began my resolution, I spent far more time with altered books than with writing. Sometimes I spent my "creative" time just *reading* about creativity or looking at magazines or sites online to spur my inspiration. Beginning, taking the initiative, is the hardest part of creating,[5] so be kind to yourself and lenient as you begin.

In addition, don't put pressure on yourself to achieve any particular goal, especially if the goal is ambitious or intimidating to you, because such expectations can result in frustration if you don't meet your goal in a session or, worse, can provoke enough anxiety to keep you from showing up at all. For example, don't set a goal date to finish a painting, a repair project, a short story, or a remodel. In the shorter term, don't go into a creativity session vowing to start and finish an outline of a script or to get all the pictures of Joey's birthday party added to his scrapbook. If any of this happens naturally, or if you get so absorbed in your work that you don't want to quit, that's great, but don't put demands on yourself beyond devoting some time daily to a creative pursuit, and you will almost undoubtedly be more successful at establishing a habit. And, though I stick with my claim that it is important to be as consistent as you can be, don't allow consistency itself to be a burden; don't beat yourself up if you miss an occasional day, because studies have shown that it does not damage the permanence of a habit to miss once in a while. There will be times that it is not possible to spend time creating—allow yourself some flexibility and grace when such times come up.

Though it isn't necessary to establish a certain *length* of time that you'll devote to daily creativity, it *is* helpful to schedule your sessions for a specific time *period*. If you pack your days with responsibilities and plans already, this might mean that you'll need to look at your calendar and schedule your sessions as though they are appointments you must keep, as important as doctor visits or meetings with clients. Doing so reminds you that the goal you've set for yourself isn't just a hopeful effort or a low-level priority, but a serious intent. If you have more flexibility, as I do, you may not schedule a

---

5. Gentry, "Overcoming the Barriers."

certain hour for creativity, but a certain segment of the day. I am definitely a morning person, so whenever possible, I set aside a morning block. Other days, when I have a full schedule of classes or a stack of papers to grade, I may not be able to have a creativity session until evening. *Ideally*, it's best to have a consistent time, if that is possible for you, because studies show that establishing a habit is easier and quicker if you don't vary the time slot you set aside for the practice you want to become habitual—and studies also show that those who do the activity in the mornings are more likely to be consistent in their efforts. This is because it is *so* easy to keep pushing back your creative time slot until "later" becomes "oops." I have found, for example, that if I take this attitude with my workouts, by later in the day I convince myself either that the vacuuming and raking leaves I did that day surely must count as exercise or I tell myself that ten o'clock at night is only eight hours from six o'clock the next day, so what does it matter if I skip a workout? Don't be me. However, if it is difficult for you to commit to a specific time slot or to have a morning session, it certainly doesn't mean you're doomed to failure. In fact, some research suggests that when we occasionally work outside of the time frames in which we are usually most productive, creative problem-solving ability is enhanced.[6]

It may also help, as it did for me, not to identify a specific or singular focus for your creativity—this way, you open yourself to a greater variety of possibilities, which keeps the time fresh, more varied, and therefore more interesting and stimulating. For example, as my earlier list of projects attests, I had several activities that kept my creative time from becoming monotonous or perfunctory. It began to be an adventure to try out new projects, especially ones involving skills I had never tested, like laying laminate flooring. I had enough different things going at any given time that the hardest part of starting a creativity session was deciding which project I wanted to work on that day.

On the other hand, persistent, ongoing work on a single project does have its own merit, instilling discipline, demonstrating commitment to a worthy pursuit, and, of course, because it results eventually in completion! You may prefer to focus your creativity, at least occasionally, in a single direction, only dabbling in other outlets when you tire of the same project or run into mental blocks. Such a concentration can result in more productivity, a more pronounced degree of improvement in your skills, and a stronger sense of identity attached to that focus. Now that

---

6. "How to Be," paras. 38–39.

I've passed that early period of needing extra motivation, I'm more content to use this latter approach. I've now settled into more of a writing mode, the focus I wanted to have from the start, and my concentration on this form of creativity has enabled me to complete several manuscripts of different lengths, genres, and styles that I can submit to a variety of markets. In addition, because I spend more time writing, my skills—clarity, organization, style, the ability to radically re-vision my work, quality of research—have improved more rapidly and substantially than my abilities in other areas, like woodworking or watercolor, in which I only dabble. Most importantly, though, the focus and time I give to my writing has solidified my identity as a writer. It has become central to my sense of self in a way that my other creative abilities have not. I truly enjoy creating altered books, improving my calligraphy techniques, and producing frame-worthy drawings; I also value the improvements in my style, technique, and imagination that are the results of the attention I have given them, but because I think of myself as a writer more than as an artist or a calligrapher, I will always devote more of my time to it.

However you determine to use or arrange your creative time—dabbling and dipping into multiple simultaneous projects or concentrating on a single endeavor; scheduling a specific time or period for your daily work or fitting it into odd nooks of time—keep as your priority above all else *consistency*. (Have I mentioned that before?) Determine to be *disciplined* and ask God to help you in your efforts, and consistent creativity *can* happen for you. I have discovered that other prods that artists sometimes tout as essential to prompting action—elements like inspiration, passion, and even motivation—are weaker and less effective than *discipline* in making creativity happen. Inspiration is exhilarating when we experience it, but it is fickle and relatively infrequent. William Faulkner said this about the importance of discipline over inspiration in his practice: "I only write when I am inspired. Fortunately, I am inspired every day at nine o'clock." Flannery O'Connor's perspective augments Faulkner's: "I don't sit at my desk because I have an idea, but in case I do." Likewise, passion for our work, or excitement that a particular project incites in us can in fact prompt us to practice creativity, yet passion, like inspiration, is sporadic and not to be counted upon. You will have many days in your lifetime that are devoid of passion, and some days when even mild interest in the work at hand is elusive.

Even the trait that most people would claim to be the most powerful in assuring consistent creativity—motivation—is inferior to the power of discipline. Motivation, in my opinion, beats out both passion and inspiration, mainly because it is self-regulated and thus more under our control. This quality makes it more useful and less erratic than either passion or inspiration. I consider myself to be highly motivated, a person who values productivity and who does not like to waste time. Motivation, along with its sidekicks of guilt and frustration, is probably what fueled my resolution to create daily, and I frequently depend on its strength to kick butt on days lacking in inspiration or passion. Still, even motivation is sometimes not enough, because it is still contingent upon emotion and mood and therefore susceptible to excuses.

Discipline, by contrast, involves determination and will power. I think discipline is what Jane Austen was describing when she allegedly wrote, "I am not at all in a humor for writing. I must write on until I am." The power of discipline is what enabled her to sit down to write despite her lacking the intrinsic motivation or even interest to do so. For example, as motivated as I usually am to get things accomplished, there are some days when I resist picking up my pen to write because I am at a transition point or working with difficult concepts that I know will make my writing time arduous, torturously slow, and frustrating. Or, to apply it to another area of my life, I am usually motivated to work out, since I know I always feel better after I do, and I know what a vital role it plays in keeping my weight down, making me stronger and more fit, and staving off the general entropy of aging. Yet despite knowing how important it is to my health, there are days when motivation stays at home with a second cup of coffee while discipline pushes me out the door.

I don't mean to disparage the value of these three impetuses. Ultimately, they all can serve as useful tools in establishing and then maintaining a consistent creative practice. Inspiration can be a flashlight to shine a light in darkness, illuminating your path; passion for your work can be a file that gives you just the edge you need to carry on; motivation is a crow bar, prying you out of your complacency and into your workshop or studio, but discipline is a hammer that can smack through most mental walls that you run against.

I have focused on our own human agency in controlling our decisions and actions because I believe that God expects us to invest in our own success and has accordingly equipped us with intelligence and strength to survive and thrive. I believe God is pleased when we take initiative, believe in ourselves, and cultivate our strengths. At the same time, however, we need to realize that we can do nothing without God. The traits, propensities, and actions that enable us to initiate success in our lives are themselves gifts to us from God. Without him, nothing was made that has been made. When our resolution or motivation or even our discipline is weak, it is not additional weakness but a strength for us to admit our need for God's help. A constant, humble awareness of our complete dependence upon God for every aspect of our existence is paradoxically the strongest stance we can have. Our creativity, as is true of all areas of our lives, grows and improves only because of God's grace, yet he allows us the pleasure and satisfaction of participating in the creative process with him, of becoming a cocreator with him. Establishing a "habitus" that privileges creativity confirms our own dedication and faithfulness to our work and, at its best, parallels our Christian commitment to the Holy Spirit's leading in our faith.[7] The consistent creative practice we cultivate enriches the beauty, truth, and meaning that we seek and give expression to through our art and will refine our *imago dei* identity.

Another suggestion for encouraging daily creative work is to have a physical space dedicated to your creativity. One advantage of having such a space is the convenience of having your materials easily accessible and your projects-in-process already laid out; this set up makes it much easier to pick up where you left off and also makes your time more productive when you have a smaller block to give to creativity. If you have to drag out all your supplies and projects every day and continually set up your work again, that might be just enough hassle to keep you from establishing a consistent practice. I'm not, of course, suggesting that you need to annex an art studio to your house in order to be successful as a creative, though if that is within your means and dreams, go for it! Having a dedicated space can mean hijacking a guest bedroom that doesn't get much traffic, clearing out a corner of a family room and bringing in a work surface and supplies to define it, or even, if every square inch of your home seems occupied and unavailable, to set up a Create Cart filled to capacity with supplies and wheel it into whatever area seems available on any given day.

Most of us, I suspect, live somewhere between these two extremes. With some careful planning and placement, most of us could set up a small area that we can devote to our creativity. For example, I started by putting

---

7. De Weese, "'White Hot Inspiration,'" para. 18.

all my art supplies in two empty but rickety bureaus that we stored in the basement. I organized them and labeled the outside of the drawers for quick access. I put all my paints and brushes in one drawer, my stamps and pads in another, my stacks of paper and boxes of scrap in another, and my tools in yet another. It was still a bit of a hassle to go downstairs every time I needed materials, though, since I didn't do my work in the basement, so eventually I arranged a different setup. I bought a small rolling cart with plastic drawers in which I store my most commonly used supplies, such as washi tape, embellishments, pencils and brush markers, and paper tags. Having my most frequently used supplies on the same floor where I created saved me many trips into the depths. Once creativity had become my habit, I stepped out more boldly: I bought a huge, rustic wooden wardrobe that I found at an antique store. When I bought it, it was in rough shape, with a splintered and broken back, no shelves, a marred finish, and a bit of a wobble. These traits, though, resulted in a stunningly low price, so I bought it, and in its first days at my home, it became the recipient of my concentrated creative attention as I forsook all my previously engaging projects to care for it. I attached new beadboard to the back, cut plywood shelves to fit, and refinished the outside, and now I have a large storage space for *all* my craft materials. The shelves are deep and wide, and I bought about two dozen matching transparent food containers at Dollar Tree to store all my supplies in. Because the containers match and stack, I have a neat and tidy display of all my materials, clearly labeled and easy to access—and all hidden from sight when not in use. The wardrobe is in one corner of a guest bedroom, and my now lowly rolling cart tucks between it and the wall, overshadowed by its Narnia-grade companion; this room has become my creative space.

    A final suggestion I'll offer that might also be an impetus for creativity is to follow your field—that is, keep informed about new techniques, products, supplies, and methods in your areas of creativity and expand your range and expertise. I, for example, have begun to read articles written by creative people that outline their process and reveal their favorite products. Doing so has introduced me to several new techniques that have enriched my work. For instance, my altered book pages prior to my research were limited to a central hand-lettered quotation embellished by mostly washi, paper ephemera, or tags. Now, I am experimenting with mixed media approaches such as using texture paste, stenciling, spray stains, collage, different gesso finishes, gel-plate printing, and embossing. A side benefit of my interest in new approaches and techniques is that it offers me the opportunity to spend more time in Hobby Lobby accumulating more art supplies, which, as I mentioned earlier, is one of the perks of the creative life! For a person who loves the crisp paper wrappers and waxy scent of a new box of crayons and who has expanded her brush marker collection to include every color imaginable, adding supplies is one of the best motivators of a continuing creative practice.

Whatever motivates you to make creativity a pronounced practice in your life—do those things. Creativity is so central to who God is that encouraging and fostering our own practice of it cannot help but draw us closer to the one who so delighted in the art of making that he gifted his ultimate creation with the same capacity. Cultivate the gift.

7

Practices that Increase Creativity

BECAUSE ALL OF US are made in the image of God, we all share his attributes, including the first trait ascribed to him in the Bible—his creativity. Artistic pursuits draw some people from an early age, and these people nurture their intrinsic creativity throughout their lives. Others, for various reasons, allow their creativity to remain dormant, unpracticed, and thus in a state of atrophy. Most probably find themselves between these two extremes: in certain periods of their lives, they may develop their creativity, then neglect it for long periods of time; sometimes they are confident in their imaginations, and at other times they question if they have any creative aptitude at all.

Regardless of where you are on this spectrum, the central purposes of this book are to convince you of your creativity, to encourage you to consistently practice it, and to assure you that you can increase the quality and originality of it. This chapter explores several ways that you can boost your creative potential, including adopting mindsets that are conducive to creativity, exposing yourself to environments that can stimulate your artistic nature, and engaging in practices and activities that will increase your creative finesse.

In my research, I was surprised and encouraged to discover that there are multiple ways to increase creativity. As I organized the information, I found I could classify most of the ideas into the categories of brain training, mindsets, environments, and activities. In reference to the first category, several sources pointed out the benefits of keeping minds nimble for creative work by challenging our brains with puzzles and word games; bodily fitness also contributes to increased creativity, so exercising both body and mind was also a recurring theme.[1] Listening to classical music, perhaps because the music itself is an expression of beauty and creativity, also stimulates creativity. And, because an environment of disorder and confusion can result in an equally chaotic mental state, keeping workspaces neat and organized can also stimulate creativity.[2] These suggestions all have a logical connection with their effects, but not all the ideas I encountered demonstrated a clear causal link. For example, one of the oddest suggestions for increasing creativity that I found recommended shifting your eyeballs from left to right for thirty seconds; the source claimed that thirty seconds of such eyeball swiveling would yield nine minutes of enhanced creativity; ostensibly, these eye motions increase the connection between the two hemispheres of the brain.[3] I'm not sure how scientifically based it is, but it's simple and free, so you might as well try it, though it might be best to limit this to times when you're alone!

Another brain-training suggestion that might at first seem equally odd is to write by hand as often as possible rather than typing into a computer, a practice that has been all but abandoned in this computer age, in which laptops and ubiquitous phones allow for always available digital notes and word processing. Yet studies confirm the many benefits of writing by hand. So convincing and overwhelming are its effects, in fact, that I require that my students take handwritten notes; towards that end, I do not allow computers in my classrooms. The benefit most pertinent to my focus here is that handwriting stimulates creativity by exercising the right side of the brain, the side responsible for creativity, since writing letters is similar to drawing.[4] Writing by hand also results in "richer and more complex" ideas, more originality, and less repetition.[5] All of these result in increased creativity in general; however, if one area of your creativity is writing, the benefits of writing by hand are especially pronounced.

Because I grew up in the BC era (Before Computers), I established a practice of writing by hand, simply because the only other option was to use a typewriter, which to me seemed a cumbersome, expensive, and

1. Fuchs, "Creativity May Be Key," paras. 23–24.
2. Ariel, "How to Be More Creative," esp. "Declutter Your Workspace."
3. "How to Be More Creative [Part 1]," paras. 35–36.
4. "20 Reasons," para. 9.
5. "16 Powerful Benefits," para. 59.

heavy choice when weighed against the lightness and freedom of carrying a notepad and pen. My choice to manually draft my writing has now been validated by extensive studies touting its advantages, so I have never made the digital transition, a decision that has enriched my writing practice in innumerable ways. My first hesitant efforts at forming words, developing thoughts, stringing together sentences and paragraphs, are impossible for me to undertake on a computer screen. I cannot compose in blue virtual space, with a frantically blinking cursor attempting to rush me along every time I pause to contemplate. Writing on paper slows my racing mind, makes me consider each word more thoughtfully, and makes my process more deliberate and intentional. I relish the way a pen slides naturally into the curve of my fingers, in a way that a computer mouse never could, and the cold mechanical screen of a computer in front of me has none of the texture and closeness of my hand resting upon the smooth grain of a sheet of paper. I need to feel the words forming on the page, the smooth glide of my pen and the quiet vibration the movement produces in the tips of my fingers. Words on paper cluster and nudge, sometimes sliding obediently across pale blue lines, other times spilling sideways down margins or wedging themselves between existing lines, piling up in messy paragraphs on the back of sheets or jumbling together on Post-it notes slapped onto the page.

There is creative benefit in having the *process* of writing laid out on the page, to see one word chosen over another, to have a record of false starts, to preserve earlier choices for reconsideration later. Lines can be crossed out—whole paragraphs even—and replaced by others, but still the first option is there, visible under the slashes. There is not the finality, the irretrievability of a block and delete command; there is the possibility of a Lazarus thought, brought back from the dead.

Written pages also preserve my writing struggles: tangible grappling with words, spreading pools of ink to mark where no words came and I was lost in thought, complicated doodles in the margins where I paused to think. Occasionally, there are fluid, breezy lines unhalted by scratched out passages or hesitantly chosen words—these are hopeful lines, flung out and towing me home, rescuing me when I feel as though I am going under. The sensory experience of writing by hand on paper nudges my writing on and adds value to the words on the page—the smoothness of the paper under the heel of my hand, the dent in my third finger from clenching my pen too tightly, the ink smudges on the outside of my pinky as it presses the words into the paper are tangible signs of my efforts. I need the decisiveness of a turned page, its soft rustle and its faint scent of trees affirming my progress. And, after the drafts are written, instead of a surreal, digital copy of my labors, I have neat stacks of legal pads that contain my dissertation, Goldenrod tablets in which I wrote my first published book, and a row of over forty pocket Moleskines that I have used over the course of years to record my observations of nature, my meditations, and my last published book—a history of my commitment to writing.

My students, of course, balk, as you may be also in reading this now, at my suggestion that they try handwriting their drafts. The most off-putting objection is that writing by hand requires that they then type the full draft, to them an unnecessary extra step. However, there is great benefit even in this, for when I type up my pages, the pace of the process allows me to get a sense of the whole and points out awkward wording, excessively long sentences, or unclear transitions in a way that simply reading it does not. Push back your hesitation on this suggestion and give it an honest try—you may discover that writing by hand revitalizes your process to such a degree that you'll never return to a computer for drafting!

In addition to these ways to stimulate brain activity, certain mindsets can also encourage creativity. One such mental state is allowing your mind to freely wander, to daydream in unfocused ways.[6] This may be the opposite of what your teachers expected of you, or it may seem antithetical to the logical, organized thinking our society values, but daydreaming, letting your mind move from subject to subject, allowing one thought to segue into another idea quite unrelated to it, can trigger unique ideas and foster a spirit of discovery. Mason Currey, author of the books *Daily Rituals* and *Daily Rituals: Women at Work*, even promotes the value of "spacing out." He advocates "doing something familiar with a kind of diffused focus that allows your mind to wander elsewhere."[7] In other words, while doing a task that requires little attention or focus, such as washing the dishes or watering the garden, allow your mind to travel wherever it wants, and go along for the ride, enjoying the spontaneous excursions it takes, taking mental (or actual) notes on any insights you stumble upon. Neil Gaiman, a prolific modern writer, also supports the idea of daydreaming as an impetus for creativity: "You get ideas from daydreaming. You get ideas from being

---

6. Fuchs, "Creativity May Be Key," para. 10.
7. Quoted in Thorp, "How Boredom Can Spark," para. 13.

bored. You get ideas all the time. The only difference between writers and other people is we notice when we're doing it."[8]

Creativity is further heightened when we are nudged out of our complacency, routine, and ordinary surroundings. Any alteration of our normal routine or environment can serve to jostle and revive creativity. If we look only in obvious places for our inspiration, we will have only obvious or usual ideas; if we look for ideas in unusual places, our creativity will reflect that freshness.[9] Even changing up our habitual patterns in small ways can sizably influence our creativity. For example, rearranging furniture, painting a room a different color, taking a different route to work, or listening to a different radio station are everyday ways to stimulate your creativity.[10] Even more influential are more dramatic shifts: take a day trip to a small town you've never visited and explore the area; buy (or even just try on!) an outfit that is very different from your usual style; try a new-to-you hairstyle; read a book in a genre you don't usually choose or by an author you are unfamiliar with; spend an afternoon people watching in a coffee shop or in a park that you've never visited. Whenever you travel, near or far, take advantage of the stimuli of new surroundings as an impetus for your creativity. For, as Jonah Lehrer says, "We travel because distance and difference are the secret tonic of creativity. When we get home, home is still the same. But something inside our minds has changed, and that changes everything."[11] While you are engaging in these experiences or soon afterwards, jot down some of your observations or new thoughts and ideas that these experiences prompted. Sometimes, fresh stimuli can have an immediate effect on your creativity, or months may pass and a memory of a past unique experience may suddenly spring to your mind and transform your day.

Most of us actively work to avoid boredom, for we regard it as deadening, especially to our creativity. However, new research is indicating that boredom is not as detrimental to our creativity as we might think, as Neil Gaiman intimated in his earlier quote. It is not that boredom in itself bolsters creativity, as Clare Thorp clarifies, but our desire to alleviate our boredom. Our brains crave activity, and in times of boredom, our minds recognize that they are receiving inadequate stimulation, so they seek to

---

8. Gaiman, "Where Do You Get," para. 17.

9. Sedgwick, "7 Ways," paras. 7–8.

10. Ariel, "How to Be More Creative," l. 125; Chung and Chang, "On Becoming Creative."

11. Shapka, "Dose of Inspiration," para. 14.

fill the empty spaces with productive mental activity. Our minds, when we are bored, are at their most active, thinking random thoughts, our synapses firing in multiple areas, all in an effort to avoid boredom. And, as I pointed out in a previous chapter, such free, unregulated thinking encourages innovation and originality.[12] For example, in a 2013 study by Sandi Mann, subjects were given the mindless task of copying phone numbers from a book; other subjects were given no task at all to complete. Immediately afterwards, both groups were told to find multiple uses for a plastic cup. The group that had been assigned the boring task came up with significantly more uses for the plastic cup. The study indicated that the more boring the initial task was, the more creative the responses afterwards were.[13] As an example of how creative our minds can be when we are trying to alleviate boredom, consider the fact that J. K. Rowling came up with the general framework and characters for her Harry Potter series on a long train ride back to her home. She had forgotten to bring anything with her to fill her hours of travel time, so the ride offered her no diversions to fill her time. Out of boredom, then, she brainstormed the plot and characters of what would become a bestselling, multi-book series.[14]

In fact, creative activity is so often the human response to boredom that psychologists express concern for the current generation, who fills every empty moment with equally empty virtual activity, flipping through social media sites, playing video games, or watching inane cat videos on YouTube. In other words, in the past when people were bored, their boredom prompted them to engage in some activity that they otherwise might not have considered, an activity that jolted them out of their listlessness and introduced a challenge or piqued their curiosity. In the digital age, however, with phones or the internet as time fillers always readily available, instead of seeking out more stimulating options, they default to just another source of boredom. With these mindless activities, boredom is not alleviated but perpetuated. Glennon Doyle comments that

> I find myself worrying most that when we hand our children phones we steal their boredom from them. As a result, we are raising a generation of writers who will never start writing, artists who will never start doodling, chefs who will never make a mess of the kitchen, athletes who will never kick a ball against a wall,

---

12. Wardle, "So, You Think."
13. Thorp, "How Boredom Can Spark," para. 8.
14. Thorp, "How Boredom Can Spark," para. 12.

musicians who will never pick up their aunt's guitar and start strumming.[15]

In addition to the many suggestions I have made that involve changing mindsets, environments, routines, and responses to boredom, there are also some specific activities that enhance and develop creativity. One such activity is walking, which stimulates the flow of ideas.[16] In fact, one study found that walking increased creativity by 60 percent, which certainly makes walking worth a try.[17] For walking to be most conducive to creativity, however, it should not be approached as though it were exercise—having an agenda or goal in walking beyond just enjoying a relaxing and reflective stroll distracts from its purpose, in this case, and the pace of exercise would likely not provide an experience that contributes to inspiration and thought, either. Rebecca Solnit, author of *Wanderlust: A History of Walking*, humorously conveys this same message when she writes that "thinking is generally thought of as doing nothing in a production-oriented culture, and doing nothing is hard to do. It's best done by disguising it as doing something, and the something closest to doing nothing is walking."[18]

Henry David Thoreau describes precisely this kind of walking, walking that provides spiritual restoration, creative stimulus, and mental enervation, in his wonderful essay called "Walking." Thoreau was an avid and consistent walker, usually logging several miles a day. Though he admitted that sometimes his walking lacked attentiveness and spiritual focus ("I am alarmed when it happens that I have walked a mile into the woods bodily, without getting there in spirit"),[19] his usual approach to walking is something we should emulate. He expresses his approach especially well in the following passage, in which he creates an etymology for the word *sauntering*, the sort of walking he usually practiced.

> I have met with but one or two persons in the course of my life who understood the art of Walking, that is, of taking walks,—who had a genius, so to speak, for *sauntering*, which word is beautifully derived "from idle people who roved about the country, in the Middle Ages, and asked charity, under pretense of going *a la Sainte Terre*," to the Holy Land, till the children exclaimed,

---

15. Doyle, *Untamed*, 158.
16. Ariel, "How to Be More Creative," l. 12.
17. Gaines, "Fostering Creativity," para. 19.
18. Quoted in Thorp, "How Boredom Can Spark," para. 15.
19. Thoreau, "Walking," 561.

"There goes a *Sainte-Terrer*," a Saunterer, a Holy-Lander. They who never go to the Holy Land in their walks, as they pretend, are indeed mere idlers and vagabonds; but they who do go there are saunterers in the good sense, such as I mean. Some, however, would derive the word from *sans terre*, without land or a home, which, therefore, in the good sense, will mean, having no particular home, but equally at home everywhere. For this is the secret of successful sauntering. He who sits still in a house all the time may be the greatest vagrant of all; but the saunterer, in the good sense, is no more vagrant that the meandering river, which is all the while sedulously seeking the shortest course to the sea.[20]

Thoreau had also mastered two other activities that are additional ways to intensify and spur creativity: spending time in nature and meditation, which he often combined with his walking. Meditation, generally defined, is setting aside time to relax and de-stress, to focus on peace and restoration of body and mind. It can, of course, take many forms—from yoga, aromatherapy, and controlled breathing exercises, most of which have their origin in Eastern religion—to pondering Scripture, slowly absorbing its truths. Meditation is usually quiet and pensive, a respite from the more hectic pattern of our everyday lives. It can be practiced alone or with others, in silence or with unobtrusive sounds or music; it can emphasize complete stillness or be more akin to Thoreau's sauntering. It can minimize stimuli or welcome sensory experience. It can be person-centered or God-centered, secular or spiritual, though I believe it is most restorative, effective, and fulfilling if it has God as its focus, for God instituted it as a practice intended to draw us nearer to him in relationship and even instituted a day for its practice—the Sabbath. If we correlate meditation with the Sabbath, its benefits, of course, go far beyond enhancing our creativity, though it is outside the range of this book to elaborate on them all.

Spending time in nature and meditation, whether practiced singly or in conjunction, can boost creativity dramatically. For example, studies reveal that spending even thirty minutes in nature measurably increases creativity[21] through nature's ability to heighten our curiosity and spur more inventive, novel thinking.[22] Likewise, meditation has also been shown to have a dramatic effect upon creativity. In a study of six hundred people who meditated, 83 percent reported that the practice had

---

20. Thoreau, "Walking," 557.
21. "How to Be More Creative [Part 1]," para. 56.
22. Ariel, "How to Be More Creative," l. 15.

increased their creativity. These findings were confirmed by three other studies involving 362 students.[23] Some of meditation's specific effects that directly contribute to increased creativity include its ability to encourage risk taking, to discern the efficacy of ideas or decisions, and to increase "field independence," or the ability to make independent decisions and to resist being swayed by others' opinions.[24]

As a companion point for all of the suggestions I have given for promoting creative growth—but particularly mandatory when walking, meditating, or spending time in nature—is that it is best if you leave technology behind. As mentioned previously, I grew up in the BC age; if you are a similar age as I, you know it is possible to live without most of the technology that is so omnipresent and controlling today. Yet some of us BCers nevertheless have become just as addicted to it as younger generations have. Carrying our phones with us wherever we go—devices that usually include text messages, email, and social media—makes us constantly available to others in multiple ways as well as perpetually distracted. Technology's accessibility and distraction rob all of these suggestions I have made of their capacity to inspire, to focus, to stir imagination, to stimulate creativity, and, most importantly, to deepen our spiritual lives. Only time will tell how much technology has stolen from us, but it is already obvious that it has a grip on us and that it will take intentional effort to resist its shallow allure in order to preserve and nourish the elements God identifies as truly essential to our human existence and thriving, things such as solitude, stillness, silence, rest, attentiveness, and spiritual perception.

One of the most frequent suggestions for developing and enlarging creativity that I came across in my research was to keep an art or idea journal. The most significant way that this increases creativity, I suspect, is by preserving ideas and inspirations that pop into our heads by writing them down.[25] Otherwise, we would undoubtedly forget most of them. Especially if ideas occur to you at random and unexpected moments during the day, a small notebook that you can carry wherever you go is indeed invaluable in preserving your ideas. Keeping a creativity notebook has a legacy of success to support it, for many great creatives such as Bruce Cantrell, Ernest Hemingway, and Leonardo DaVinci kept such notebooks. DaVinci used his notebook to write down questions he had, to sketch out designs for his

23. Fuchs, "Creativity May Be Key," para. 17.
24. Fuchs, "Creativity May Be Key," paras. 18–19.
25. Scott, "23 Good Work Habits," paras. 99–108

inventions, and to create studies for his paintings.[26] Beyond preservation of our ideas, however, are several additional useful purposes for keeping a creativity notebook. One purpose is to create to-do lists, either outlining necessary steps or stages involved in a single project, compiling a list of creative projects you would like to explore, or listing various elements you would like to include in a single project. For example, I wanted to make a side table made from a cross section of a tree trunk and supported by a stack of books, so in my notebook I made both a list of the supplies I would need and the steps of the process. Another list recorded several projects I wanted to complete in a certain week: move my art supplies into a single cabinet, prep a new altered book, write another section of my book. Another list collected ideas and techniques I could use for altered books; as I read about other artists' techniques, examine art journal examples online, or brainstorm my own ideas, I add items to the list to try later.

A creativity notebook is also a good place to take notes on different things you are researching. Your research could involve viewing a tutorial on how to use resists with watercolor, how to miter the corners of a homemade wooden box, or how to restore a piece of furniture. Alternately, for writing projects especially, you might need to deepen your knowledge about a particular topic, consulting published articles and citing others who have previously written on the subject, as I did when I was preparing to write this book. Sometimes, though, it is not a book project but only an eager curiosity to learn more about something that intrigues us which prompts our research—curiosity and attentiveness, as I pointed out in chapter 3, are hallmarks of a creative person, and we should follow our curiosity wherever it takes us. For example, I had been sitting on the porch in the mornings, watching hummingbirds as they furiously fought off other hummers, defending their right to be the exclusive sippers at each station. So intent were they in their defense, however, that they themselves rarely had time to drink. This behavior piqued my interest in learning more about the birds. My research yielded dozens of fascinating facts about hummingbirds that were new to me and which confirmed God's design. I ended up using that collection of facts for an altered book page, but even if I had not, I know that the research itself stimulated my creativity and enlarged my attentiveness to God's creativity as well. More recently, I have been researching how to make homemade art products for multimedia art, a new interest of mine,

---

26. Gaines, "Fostering Creativity," para. 43.

so my notebook now includes recipes for gesso and embossing ink and instructions for making gel plates.

Another use for a notebook is as a repository of inspirational quotations. I have a huge collection of quotations from a variety of artists, authors, inventors, and other creative types that I have culled from *Pinterest*, magazines, devotionals, and leisure reading that I frequently consult. I integrate some of these quotations into my altered books and calligraphy; others remain in my notebook to provide inspiration and motivation when my own stock of either wanes. Some quotations remind me that the work of creativity is often arduous, and it comforts me to know that even well-established creatives can sometimes still struggle as I do. My notebook also includes Scripture that celebrates divine and human creativity or that just reminds me of where my priorities should lie. Some people use their notebooks to doodle in, a practice that actually reduces the levels of the stress hormone cortisol in the body[27] and seems to stimulate creative thought.

An element of a creative notebook that Christian creatives would especially want to include is meditations and prayers. Because as Christian subcreators our creativity often functions as an act of worship, bringing praise to God, a large part of our creative process should be to submit our creative freedom to God's control, to maintain a humble posture before God, and to continually assess whether our art is honoring to God and in line with his moral principles. My meditations and prayers sometimes address these issues directly; at other times, the connection is more oblique. For example, I often meditate in nature and describe what I am observing, adding any spiritual insights God gives to me. Sometimes these meditations suggest a new direction for my art or writing; other times the notes I take on things I'm observing in nature or an insight that God reveals to me becomes a starter seed for a later essay or blog post. Intentionally focusing on spiritual matters as I create keeps me rightly focused by reminding me that my creativity is a gift from God that I want to offer back to him in gratitude.

One of the most satisfying purposes of a creativity notebook, however, is the record it becomes of the progress you are making as you invest more and more time in developing your creativity. For me, my reaction to this record is satisfying with a healthy dose of embarrassment on the side. It's painful at times to look back on early efforts and see how tenuous or flawed they were; embarrassment at early efforts, however, almost certainly indicates that the quality of the work has improved, so ultimately a creativity

---

27. Ariel, "How to Be More Creative," l. 58.

notebook is tangible evidence of your growth as an artist and of God's help as you grope towards realizing more of your *imago dei* potential.

Ultimately, of course, your creativity notebook can include anything you choose—anything that can encourage your creative pursuits. A creativity notebook can itself become an expression of creativity. I have seen working notebooks that were themselves works of art, full of wonderful sketches, experiments with color and different media—a travel journal of creative journeys. Having your notebook with you wherever you go is a constant reminder of your commitment to your artistic identity.

Because many creatives tend to do their work in solitude—I certainly camp out here—another suggestion that can nudge you out of your seclusion and can actually boost creative activity and expertise is to share your work in a creative community. Renaissance art was the product of communities of artists gathering around a master, with apprentices contributing collectively to a master's work.[28] DaVinci, for example, was a student of Verrocchio, and by most standards he exceeded his master's abilities due in part to Verrocchio's selfless investment in him. Later artistic communities, like the self-named Lost Generation of the 1920s, a group of expatriates who relocated to Paris and established an artistic salon, put less emphasis on the master/student relationship. Instead, they tended to contribute equally to the assessment of each other's works, providing suggestions, criticism, and encouragement to each other. This group included such American writers as Earnest Hemingway, Gertrude Stein, and F. Scott Fitzgerald and artists such as Picasso and Matisse.

Such collaborative communities or mentor relationships, of course, existed in biblical times, well before either of these well-known groups, and each had its own character, purpose, and field of interest. In Exodus, for example, the workers who collectively constructed the tabernacle could be considered such a group, with all sharing their talents and improving in their art through their collaboration. A quite different and more intimate biblical example might be Elijah's mentorship of Elisha, his successor, and even the early church, with their communal sharing and frequent gathering for worship in an era of persecution is another, later example.[29]

Groups such as these, whether one on one or involving great numbers, can provide many benefits to those who seek them out. Mentor/mentee relationships can be the most influential, since the dynamic is usually more

---

28. Card, *Scribbling in the Sand*, 108.
29. Card, *Scribbling in the Sand*, 108.

personal and intensive, fostering an intimate knowledge of each other's art and allowing very specific input on the part of the mentor, but larger groups can also be quite valuable in offering constructive criticism that can improve our work.[30] At the university where I teach, both of the professors in my department who teach creative writing classes utilize a workshop model, in which students share their work with each other and offer helpful suggestions for improvement. This approach can be somewhat intimidating, but it has also proved to be ultimately stimulating and productive.

Being part of a creative group can also provide accountability: when others expect us to create and are eager to see our work, this can provide the motivation we need to be consistent in our practice. In fact, even if the group members never comment on each other's art, but gather only for the pleasure of mingling with fellow creators, people who value art as much as we do,[31] meeting with others can confirm the value of what we do and can prod us to produce better art. Without engaging in a creative community to some degree, we are in danger of creating in a void, with no audience, no accountability, no encouragement, and no outside perspective that can assess our work more objectively.

Additionally, sharing work with others and surrounding ourselves with a variety of styles, media, and messages of others' art can inspire us to try new things, to experiment and to enlarge our own repertoire.[32] Exposing ourselves to a wider range of artistic forms and admiring novel techniques present us with a smorgasbord of ideas to emulate, ideas that, if we had created alone, we could not have conceived of. Especially in the fall, my husband and I make the rounds of the festivals in Indiana, most of which feature craft vendors. It is inspiring to me to see what others are doing artistically, and often it stirs my imagination to rethink my own projects. For example, I had put battery-operated twinkle lights and elements like pine cones and small ornaments in Mason jars for Christmas decorations, but at a festival, I saw someone who had mounted them on barn shingles and attached a hook for hanging objects, which enhanced not only the beauty of the jars but their functionality also. Seeing others' art also often inspires me to try my hand at it myself—I added calligraphy to my artistic practice after a crafter's display of hand-lettered dictionary pages awed me. And I always

---

30. Card, *Scribbling in the Sand*, 111.
31. Chung and Chang, "On Becoming Creative."
32. Sedgwick, "7 Ways."

come away with my appreciation for art heightened and my excitement for creating stoked when I visit craft shows or museums.

Finally, if the creative groups we participate in are Christian ones, they can help us to stay true to the theology of creativity that I described in chapter 6. When we create for the glory of God, we submit ourselves to higher standards and loftier purposes; maintaining a commitment to truth, beauty, and goodness is difficult work, especially in a world that increasingly devalues the things of God, even mocking our stance and belittling our value as artists if we refuse to allow our art to reflect darkness, hopelessness, and despair, or if we desire for our art to reflect something higher than the prevailing culture. A Christian creative community, then, can provide the same benefits as a vibrant church: strength in numbers, the comforting affirmation of our values from like-minded people, and an atmosphere of love, acceptance, and belonging not based on our level of talent or success but on our shared faith in Christ and our desire to honor him through our creative output.[33]

Despite my awareness of the many benefits of community upon my art, I must admit that, for me, it is not a natural impulse to be part of a community but a practice I must intentionally push myself towards. I deeply value being alone, so I create almost entirely in solitude. I thrive artistically in the quiet, meditative environment that creating by myself offers. I especially recoil from opportunities to promote my work, like book signings, author talks, or art shows, though all these are activities publishers expect their authors to engage in. I switch into Emily Dickinson mode at such times: my shy factor doubles, as does my awkwardness in promoting or even speaking about my own work, though I have not yet taken up the habit of wearing all white clothing.

If you are like me in this regard, a way for you to receive some of the benefits I've listed here without becoming suddenly social is to visit art galleries, take courses to learn new skills and to add new areas of creativity to your practice, follow creativity blogs, watch *YouTube* tutorials, and, of course, check out *Pinterest* on a regular basis (yes, there are some positive uses of technology!) These should not entirely replace interaction with real people, but in my experience, they provide ways to learn from other people and to ease into social situations that otherwise might cause trepidation. The important thing is to experience all you can of the wonderful creativity

---

33. Card, *Scribbling in the Sand*, 113.

that abounds in this world, to learn from it and appreciate it, and to determine to make your life itself a work of art.

A practice that can involve several of the conducive-to-creativity activities that I've mentioned in this chapter—altering your usual routine or surroundings, meditation, being in nature, sharing your work, walking—is going on a personal or communal retreat. A retreat can provide a much-needed jump start for a new project that seems intimidating or can resuscitate a long-term project that is losing momentum or energy. Alternately, if you are working on something that you're excited about and are directing your energies toward, a retreat can intensify your productivity. Planning for a retreat in and of itself speaks to the value that you place upon your creative life and reminds you that you are an artist willing to invest in your work. Julia Cameron, a writer who established her reputation with the book *The Artist's Way*, also prioritizes the value of retreats, making "artist dates," as well as morning pages, mandatory features of her well-known beginners' program in creativity.[34]

Though it would be lovely to have the money and the time to create an ideal context for every retreat—a "destination" event, with comfortable accommodations, perhaps, and several days to devote to your craft, in all likelihood, this is out of range for most of us, at least to indulge in on a regular basis. Thankfully, retreats need not be elaborate or long to be effective breaks. A block of several hours spent somewhere outside of your usual surroundings is usually sufficient enough to qualify as a retreat. Personal retreats are the simplest to arrange, since they involve coordinating with no one's schedule but your own, are planned to your specific tastes, interests, and location, and can be extremely economical. For example, I took one of my retreats at a state park about thirty-five minutes from my house—not a new destination, but a place I visit infrequently enough that it still felt like a fresh environment. I packed some snacks in a backpack, along with my notebook and my research notes, and immediately upon arrival, I left the trail and tramped about in the woods until I found a quiet and relatively secluded spot to hang my hammock. For the hours I was there, I remained in my hammock, writing in my notebook and occasionally digging into my backpack for a snack. It was one of the first truly warm days of spring, which was in itself inspiring and invigorating enough to spur me towards productivity. As I worked, the shadows lengthened, and the cooler air of

---

34. Cameron, *Artist's Way*.

dusk signaled the end of the retreat, so I stuffed my *Eno* back into its bag and drove home with a full chapter drafted in my notebook.

Sometimes my private retreats involve spending just a morning or an afternoon in a relatively quiet coffee shop, far enough from home that no one knows me. A day in a library, tucked into a corner or set up on an upper floor, virtually assures an undisturbed, quiet block of creative time. I would love to have an occasional weekend retreat, by myself, in a little cabin or in a state park lodge, where I could punctuate my creative times with walks on trails or some time spent paddleboarding or soaking up the sun, but so far I have not done something so extravagant. Frankly, I sometimes consider it a retreat just to be able to go to my cabin with a thermos of coffee, my little Morkie Spunky, and a packed lunch and spend the day there, breaking up my writing sessions with a short walk into the ravine, or by spreading my camp blanket on the ground so I can lie looking up at the trees swaying in the breeze and the sun flashing between the leaves.

If, however, interactions with others are more effective in stimulating your creativity, or if you, like me, need to push yourself towards communal interaction with your art, you might sign up for a scheduled retreat that a third party has organized, or you could invite a few friends to join you for a retreat that you plan. One communal retreat experience could be to attend a retreat or workshop that focuses on your area of creativity. Some of my creative writing colleagues, for example, have applied for selection at writing retreats—not Bread Loaf or Yaddo, maybe, but well-organized retreats that offer group sessions, special speakers, time for independent work on their projects, and sometimes assessments from other retreat attendees or specialists. Sometimes, local colleges, women's organizations, extension offices, or churches host conferences with creativity foci—for example, gourmet cooking, cake decorating, oil painting, mixed media, Christmas cards, and organic gardening are some of the weekend workshops I have seen offered by local businesses.

Another option is to plan a low-key retreat yourself and invite a few of your friends to enjoy it with you. This alternative offers the advantage of the participants all knowing each other, your being in charge of the venue, focus, and schedule, and the cost of the event being lower for you, especially if you charge participants a small fee for supplies, ask them to provide their own meals, and if you can secure a venue that will not charge rent—check with your church, community buildings, or areas used by local service organizations like Lions Club or Kiwanis. You can choose a

PRACTICES THAT INCREASE CREATIVITY

single focus for the retreat—such as making homemade cards—or take a broader approach and work on multiple projects of various types, contingent on the length of your retreat. My niece Callie meets with a small group of friends once a month, with each month featuring a different project. The women all take turns hosting the get-together, and that month's hostess chooses the creative angle. One unique craft the women shared was making their own vanilla extract by filling small, beautiful bottles with vodka and soaking vanilla pods in the liquor. They then decorated their bottles with raffia, twine, ribbon, and other materials.

It is heartening to know that the innate creativity that each one of us possesses can be expanded and nurtured in so many ways, from adopting simple practices such as writing by hand, exposing ourselves to new stimuli, or limiting exposure to technology. We can realize even greater gains through committing to ongoing, lifelong practices like walking, meditating, or spending time in nature. Due to their explicitly creative focus, keeping a creativity notebook and engaging with other creative people, sharing ideas and learning from each other, are practices even more effective in stimulating your creative potential. Though all of us, because we are made in the image of God, share his creative nature, we have a wide range of aptitudes or interests, as well as huge variations in areas of practice. This variety assures, by God's plan, that each of us has something valuable to contribute to the world that will expand the beauty, truth, and meaning that God set into motion at the moment of creation. And, to guarantee the sustenance and growth of our creativity, God has provided almost limitless opportunities for the expansion and development of our creativity. This potential rustles within us all, an eager spirit wanting to express itself. Give it voice.

8

Art the Father Loves

When my children were very young, all of them drew pictures. Sometimes I would watch them at work, smiling at their effort and concentration, yet also at the joy that they put into their creations. Kelsey, our oldest and always the perfectionist, nearly skipped the stage that most children go through when their stick figures lack a neck and instead have their arms protruding from the sides of their head and when torsos appear as a second circle under the head, like snowballs on a snowman. Her figures wore clothes and had arms that included elbows, and it wasn't long before she was dimensionally shading the pictures in her coloring books. Nathanael, our only boy, was fascinated by machines early on; his drawings by age eight were of stunningly complicated inventions, complete with pulleys, levers, and interlocking gears, and all designed for a specific purpose—to make the fastest go cart, to design a box with a dial that would travel back and forward in time; or to create a way to haul food up to him in a treehouse. His drawings filled pages of spiral notebooks. His penciled lines pressed hard into the paper, producing an embossed reverse image on the back side of each sheet. Faith and Caitlyn, our twins, both loved to draw and color. Art sets of markers, pads of paper, new boxes of crayons, or coloring books they could paint with water that would magically transform into color upon contact were their favorite gifts. They would lie for hours on their stomachs, feet up in the air, giggling and comparing pictures and contributing to each other's work. They showed more joy in the process than either Kelsey or Nathanael.

Nearly always, I and my husband Jim would be the recipients of their art. When they completed a picture, they would run to me, excited to give me something that they had made and were proud of and eager to see my equally excited response. And, of course, I gave them what they expected: exclamations of delight, tight hugs and head kisses, praise for the beautiful purple hair on a stick figure or the cleverness of using rubber bands instead of ropes on a pulley so it would have more boing ability or the cheeriness of a whole page of pink daisies. My compliments weren't feigned—I *did* love their art, the joyful way they used every crayon in the box, the uniqueness of each child's style, the love that prompted them to give their pictures to me. I hardly noticed if their picture people lacked necks or if every dress looked like a triangle or if they used colors that didn't appear in nature. Our refrigerator became an art gallery for several years with a constantly revolving display. Not every masterpiece made the fridge, but when one didn't, it wasn't ever an aesthetic judgement but only a space issue.

As they got older, their drawings, of course, improved. Kelsey became a studio art minor in college, and again, I was at the receiving end of many of her projects: a typographical picture of Thoreau's cabin "drawn" with the words from *Walden*, a self-portrait, a ring she designed herself that ended up using far more silver than she could afford. Nathanael, when he was probably ten or eleven, presented me with a chunk of tree branch on which he had written "I love you," the words burned into the wood by focusing the rays of the sun onto the wood with a magnifying glass; it is on a shelf in my office, and it would be the first thing I would grab if the room was on fire. In his high school ceramics class, he sculpted both a model of a broken, fragmented light bulb and a rendition of the five-headed beast of the apocalypse from the description given in Revelation; the latter would *not* be the first thing I would grab in the event of a fire, but his art instructor entered the former in an art competition. Faith spent countless hours on a handmade book that she designed for me, especially treasured because she knew me well enough to feature one of my favorite authors. She crafted even the book itself, sewing the signatures together and making the cover from fabric-covered book board. Within the pages, she reproduced some of my favorite quotations from Thoreau using her early calligraphy style and illustrated them with drawings in watercolor, pencil, markers, and ink. Caitlyn's artistry exhibited itself best in her eye for photographic composition. She possessed a natural instinct for foregrounding her predominant subject, using light and shade, and intuitively choosing an interesting angle or perspective. By this point in time, the *quality* of their work was vastly superior to their childhood attempts, and though I was proud of and acknowledged their talent, I'm not sure my appreciation and delight in the art itself was any greater than for their earlier efforts. I treasure both their childhood and adult art and would not trade any of them for an original Rembrandt.

If my point isn't clear to you already, I believe these stories about my children's artistic histories illustrate well the formation of our creativity and how God responds to our efforts.

My stories aren't unique in the least. I'm sure that as you read my account, you were smiling and nodding, my stories helping you remember almost identical ones from your own children or your own childhood. And this is the point. God gifts *all* of us with a measure of his own creativity, and especially in childhood, that creativity often expresses itself through the arts. As children, we simply create, freely and unselfconsciously, delighting in the process, enjoying the experimentation, giving no thought at all to whether or not we have talent and never comparing the quality of our art to anyone else's. We also have little sense of ownership of our art or reticence to share it with anyone. This confirms Pablo Picasso's position, which claims that "every child is an artist. The problem is how to remain an artist once we grow up."[1]

Later, other interests may crowd out and replace what seems to me a universal interest in creativity and the arts, but the *potential* is still there; if children continue to practice art, they will improve, and *all* of them, I believe, could show giftedness in some form of artistic expression. Instead, they begin to notice that someone else's skill is better than theirs or that baseball is a more exciting (or maybe even a more culturally encouraged) pastime than art or, worst of all, someone has criticized or mocked their art, putting a quick end to their pursuit of creativity. The end result of this shift is that most people, globally, do not consider themselves creative. In a study by Adobe, a manufacturer of creative software, that involved 5,000 people in the US, UK, Japan, Germany, and France, only 41 percent considered themselves creative. This relatively low percentage is skewed somewhat by the US's numbers; Americans were far more likely to consider themselves creative than the other countries in the study; still, even with this imbalance, the global average was only 41 percent. Despite their conviction that they were uncreative, though, the respondents still seemed to believe in their *ability* to be creative,

---

1. Martelle, "Picasso and the Art," para. 2.

since only 25 percent felt they were realizing their creative potential, suggesting they felt they had more room for growth.[2]

God, like a loving father, wants us to remember and to reconnect with our childhood expression of creativity. He does not compare our expertise to his other children, like Matisse or Dillard or Bach, and find us wanting. He is delighted with our efforts, and not even because our efforts are always delightful, but because he delights in us. He wants us to retain the joy and freedom and expression and innovation and unconventionality and fun that once were the outcomes of artistic creativity for us and are still the qualities of creativity for him.

Most of all, he wants us to remember that our creativity is his gift to us, an attribute of his own that he shares with us. Even if our stick figures still have arms growing out of their cheeks, he loves what we produce. If we practice our art for God, an audience of one who is the Only One, it will always have purpose and value and significance to the one for whom we create it. In heaven, God's refrigerator is gigantic, and you can be sure that your drawing is on it.

---

2. Develo, "Less Than Half," fig. 1.

Bibliography

Acuff, Jon. "Be Brave Enough to Be Bad at Something New," *YouTube*, June 22, 2021. https://www.youtube.com/watch?v=KoxYiUNeWkk.

Adams, Scott. *Stick to Drawing Comics, Monkey Brain! Cartoonist Ignores Helpful Advice.* New York: Portfolio, 2007.

Animalogic. "The Platypus: The King of Weirdos." *YouTube*, August 21, 2020. https://www.youtube.com/watch?v=7-_b73LX8IY.

Ariel, Jade. "How to Be More Creative." *Jade's Journey* (blog), n.d. https://jadesjourneyblog.com/how-to-boost-creativity/.

Bertsch, Carolina. "Can Trees and Animals Show Empathy and and Altruism?" *Peace Blog*, September 7, 2018. https://blog.peacerevolution.net/can-trees-and-animals-show-empathy-and-altruism/.

Biographics. "Vincent Van Gogh: The Humble Genius." *YouTube*, January 10, 2020. https://www.youtube.com/watch?v=wI2i5ca1RT4.

"The Blue Whale's Heart | Size, Weight, Blood Vessels, and Other Facts." *Whale Facts* (blog), n.d. https://www.whalefacts.org/blue-whale-heart/.

Britt, Robert Roy. "13 Incredible, Lucky Earth Facts." *Live Science*, July 12, 2012. https://www.livescience.com/21546-earth-facts.html.

Brown, Brian. "Series Introduction: The Centric Genius." *Anselm Society* (blog), February 10, 2020. https://www.anselmsociety.org/blog/2020/1/19/sample-centric-genius-post-b5cjh.

Bureau of Labor Statistics. "Time Spent in Leisure and Sports Activities." https://www.bls.gov/opub/ted/2023/time-spent-in-leisure-and-sports-activities-2022.htm.

Cameron, Julia. *The Artist's Way: A Spiritual Path to Higher Creativity.* New York: Tarcher-Perigree, 1992.

Card, Michael. *Scribbling in the Sand: Christ and Creativity.* Westmont, IL: InterVarsity, 2002.

Carlson, Eric. "Why Beauty Is Important for Our Lives and Our Cities." *Medium*, March 4, 2019. https://medium.com/@ericcarlson/why-beauty-is-important-f0253d0e409f.

Carver, Courtney. "Why Creativity Is So Important." Cheltenham Design Festival, Oct. 2, 2019. https://web.archive.org/web/20200929180858/https://cheltdesignfestival.org/why-creativity-is-so-important/.

CBC Kids News. "The Platypus Just Got Weirder: Turns Out They Glow in the Dark." *CBC Kids News*, November 26, 2020. https://www.cbc.ca/kidsnews/post/platypuses-just-got-weirder-turns-out-they-glow-in-the-dark#.

Chandler, Steve. *100 Ways to Motivate Yourself: Change Your Life Forever*. Rev. ed. Pompton Plains, NJ: Career Press, 2001. https://ebook-mecca.com/online/100%20Ways%20to%20Motivate%20Yourself%20Change%20Your%20Life%20Forever.pdf.

Chepkemoi, Joyce. "How Many Fish Live in the Ocean?" https://www.worldatlas.com/articles/how-many-fish-are-there-in-the-ocean.html#:~:text.

Ching-Teng, Yao, et al. "Positive Effects of Art Therapy on Depression and Self-esteem of Older Adults in Nursing Homes." *Social Work in Health Care* 58 (2019) 324–38. https://doi.org/10.1080/00981389.2018.1564108.

Christensen, Tanner. "What Causes Creativity?" https://www.pinterest.es/pin/314266880220743126/.

Chung, Bryan, and Brian Chang. "On Becoming Creative: Practical Tips from Alabaster's Co-Founders." *Alabaster* (blog), n.d. https://www.alabasterco.com/blogs/the-journal/on-becoming-creative-practical-tips-from-alabasters-co-founders.

Clarkson, Joel. "How Creativity Connects Us with the Creator." *Relevant*, November 3, 2021. https://relevantmagazine.com/faith/three-ways-creativity-connects-the-created-with-the-creator/.

Clear, James. "Creativity: How to Unlock your Hidden Creative Genius." *James Clear* (blog), n.d. https://jamesclear.com/creativity.

———. "Make More Art: The Health Benefits of Creativity." *James Clear* (blog), n.d. https://jamesclear.com/make-more-art.

"Climbing Gourami." *Real Monstrosities: A Journey amongst the Weird, the Wonderful, and the Downright Ugly of the Natural World* (blog), October 2, 2017. http://www.realmonstrosities.com/2013/10/climbing-gourami.html.

Cloud, David. "The Woodpecker's Design." *Way of Life Literature* (blog), February 27, 2018. https://www.wayoflife.org/reports/the_woodpeckers_design.php.

Cohut, Maria. "What Are the Health Benefits of Being Creative?" *Medical News Today*, February 16, 2021. https://www.medicalnewstoday.com/articles/320947.

Connolly, Jim. "Art Is Not What You See, but What You Make Others See." *Creative Thinking Hub* (blog), August 19, 2013. https://www.creativethinkinghub.com/art-is-not-what-you-see-but-what-you-make-others-see/.

Daley, Jason. "Deep-Sea Snail Builds Its Own Ironclad Suit of Armor. But Even That Can't Protect It From Ocean Mining." *Smithsonian Magazine*, July 25, 2019. https://www.smithsonianmag.com/smart-news/deep-sea-snail-iron-shell-first-creature-declared-endangered-ocean-mining-180972727/.

Delistraty, Cody. "A Neurological Defense of Aestheticism: Why Our Brains Crave Beauty." *Thought Catalog* (blog), May 6, 2014. https://thoughtcatalog.com/cody-delistraty/2014/05/a-neurological-defense-of-aestheticism-why-our-brains-crave-beauty/.

Develo, Todd Henry. "Less Than Half of People Would Describe Themselves as Creative." *Idea to Value: The Community for Creativity and Innovation* (blog), January 12, 2022. https://www.ideatovalue.com/lead/nickskillicorn/2022/01/less-than-half-of-people-would-describe-themselves-as-creative/#:~:text.

BIBLIOGRAPHY

De Weese, Alexis. "'White Hot Inspiration': Creative Impulse in Light of Divine Encounters." *Transpositions: Theology, Imagination, and the Arts* (blog), July 6, 2021. https://www.transpositions.co.uk/white-hot-inspiration-creative-impulse-in-light-of-divine-encounter/.

Dickinson, Emily. "This Was a Poet—It Is That." *American Poems* (blog), July 2, 2002. https://www.americanpoems.com/poets/emilydickinson/this-was-a-poet-it-is-that/.

Dillard, Annie. *An American Childhood*. New York: HarperPerennial, 1987.

———. *Holy the Firm*. New York: HarperPerennial, 1977.

———. *Living by Fiction*. New York: HarperPerennial, 1988.

———. *Pilgrim at Tinker Creek*. New York: HarperPerennial, 1988.

———. *The Writing Life*. New York: HarperPerennial, 1989.

Doyle, Glennon. *Untamed*. New York: Dial Books, 2020.

Estudio Arkano. "Your Mind Will Collapse if You Try to Imagine This | Universe Size Comparison." *YouTube*, December 31, 2019. https://www.youtube.com/watch?v=TXfOzhZGtNw.

Field Museum. "Woodpeckers Show Signs of Possible Brain Damage, but That Might Not Be a Bad Thing." *Science Daily*, February 2, 2018. https://www.sciencedaily.com/releases/2018/02/180202140910.htm.

Flanders Marine Institute. "Number of Marine Species." https://www.coastalwiki.org/wiki/Number_of_marine_species.

Fosbury, Robert A. E., and Glen Jeffery. "Reindeer Eyes Seasonally Adapt to Ozone-Blue Arctic Twilight by Tuning a Photonic Tapetum Lucidum." *Proceedings of the Royal Society B* 289 (2022) n.p. https://royalsocietypublishing.org/doi/10.1098/rspb.2022.1002.

Frank, Priscilla. "Study Says Making Art Reduces Stress, Even If You Suck at It." *Huffington Post*, June 16, 2016. https://www.huffpost.com/entry/study-says-making-art-reduces-stress_n_576183ece4b09c926cfdccac.

Fuchs, Matt. "Creativity May Be Key to Healthy Aging. Here Are Ways to Stay Inspired." *Washington Post*, July 12, 2021. https://www.washingtonpost.com/lifestyle/wellness/creativity-may-be-key-to-healthy-aging-here-are-ways-to-stay-inspired/2021/07/10/679e20fc-e0e1-11eb-9f54-7eee10b5fcd2_story.html.

Gaiman, Neil. "Where Do You Get Your Ideas?" *Cool Stuff* (blog), n.d. https://neilgaiman.com/Cool_Stuff/Essays/Essays_By_Neil/Where_do_you_get_your_ideas%3F.

Gaines, Jeffrey. "Fostering Creativity: 12 Strategies to Boost Creative Skills." *Positive Psychology*, August 13, 2020. https://positivepsychology.com/creativity/.

Gentry, Geoff. "Overcoming the Barriers to Creating: Lessons in Beginning Again and Again and Again." *Alabaster* (blog), n.d. https://www.alabasterco.com/blogs/articles/overcoming-the-barriers-to-creating.

———. "A Theology of Making." *Alabaster* (blog), n.d. https://www.alabasterco.com/blogs/articles/a-theology-of-making.

Gibbs, Sarah M. "Question of the Week: Why Are Sea Sponges Considered Animals?" *Researchers in Museums* (blog), May 29, 2018. https://blogs.ucl.ac.uk/researchers-in-museums/2018/05/29/question-of-the-week-why-are-sea-sponges-considered-animals/.

GirlScientist. "Watch: This Brilliant Girl Dances for Her Supper." *The Guardian*, July 18, 2015. https://www.theguardian.com/science/grrlscientist/2015/jul/18/watch-this-brilliant-bird-dances-for-her-supper#.

Harvey, Ailsa. "How Many Stars Are in the Universe?" *Space* (blog), February 11, 2022. https://www.space.com/26078-how-many-stars-are-there.html.

Haun, Stephanie. "Happy Accidents: What Bob Ross Can Teach Us about the World." *The Smart Set* (blog), April 29, 2019. https://www.thesmartset.com/we-dont-make-mistakes-just-happy-little-accidents/.

Heintz, Elizabeth C., et al. "Determinants of Missed Games Following Concussions in the NFL." *Frontiers in Sports and Active Living* 2 (2020) n.p. https://www.ncbi.nlm.nih.gov/pmc/articles/PMC7739784/.

"Here's Why You Should Be Proud of Your Trashy First Draft." *Dot and Dash* (blog), May 14, 2020. https://www.dotanddashllc.com/post/here-s-why-you-should-be-proud-of-your-trashy-first-draft.

Hickey, Pat. "What I Learned from You, the Readers." *Reno Gazette Journal*, September 20, 2023. https://www.rgj.com/story/opinion/2023/09/20/what-i-learned-from-you-the-readers/70903801007/.

"Hippo." https://animals.sandiegozoo.org/animals/hippo.

Hopkins, Gerard Manley. "God's Grandeur." Poetry Foundation, https://www.poetryfoundation.org/poems/44395/gods-grandeur.

Howard, Thomas. "On Evil in Art." *Christianity Today*, December 17, 1971. https://www.christianitytoday.com/ct/1971/december-17/on-evil-in-art.html.

"How Big Is Blue Whale's Tongue?" https://www.scifacts.net/animals/blue-whale-tongue-size/.

"How to Be More Creative [Part 1: Your Actions]." *3D Success* (blog), n.d. https://3dsuccess.org/be-more-creative-actions/.

Huang, Chuan-Yung, et al. "The Effects of Group Art Therapy on Adolescents' Self-Concept and Peer Relationship: A Mixed-Method Study," *New Directions for Child and Adolescent Development* (2021) 75–92. https://doi.org/10.1002/cad.20435.

"Interview with Kate Mosse." *Writers and Artists* (blog), n.d. https://web.archive.org/web/20130811165515/https://www.writersandartists.co.uk/writers/advice/43/a-writers-toolkit/interviews-with-authors/interview-with-kate-mosse.

Jacobson, D. J. "Finding vs. Making Time" *D. J. Jacobson* (blog), n.d. https://djjacobson.com/finding-vs-making-time/?v=4326ce96e26c.

Jehovah's Witnesses. "The Living Planet." https://www.jw.org/en/library/books/was-life-created/the-living-planet/.

"Johann Sebastian Bach." *Christianity Today*, n.d. https://www.christianitytoday.com/history/people/musiciansartistsandwriters/johann-sebastian-bach.html.

Kean, Sam. "Sweating Blood." *Distillations Magazine*, July 29, 2018. https://sciencehistory.org/stories/magazine/sweating-blood/.

Leith, James A., ed. *Symbols in Life and Art: The Royal Society of Canada*. Kingston, Ont.: McGill Queen's Press, 1987.

L'Engle, Madeleine. *Walking on Water: Reflections on Faith and Art*. Wheaton, IL: Shaw, 2001.

"Leo Frideric Handel." *Christianity Today*, n.d. https://www.christianitytoday.com/history/people/musiciansartistsandwriters/george-frideric-handel.html.

Lewis, C. S. *Mere Christianity*. N.p.: Touchstone, 1996.

Liesch, Barry, and Thomas Finley. "The Biblical Concept of Creativity: Scope, Definition, Criteria." *Journal of Psychology and Theology* 12 (1984) 188–97. https://journals.sagepub.com/doi/abs/10.1177/009164718401200303.

BIBLIOGRAPHY

Lindsley, Art. "Why Your Creativity Matters to God." *Institute for Faith, Work, and Economics* (blog), June 19, 2019. https://tifwe.org/why-your-creativity-matters-to-god/.

Lockerbie, Bruce. *The Timeless Moment: Creativity and the Christian Faith.* Katy, TX: Cornerstone, 1980.

Loewen, Jaycie. "Football Concussions: Prevention, Diagnosis, and Recovery." *Cognitive FX* (blog), April 5, 2023. https://www.cognitivefxusa.com/blog/football-concussion-prevention-and-recovery.

Lott, Bret. "The Artist and the City, or, Some Random Thoughts on Why We Are Here." In *Letters and Life: On Being a Writer, on Being a Christian,* 33–45. Wheaton, IL: Crossway, 2013.

———. "A Home, a House: On Writing and Rejection." In *Before We Get Started: A Practical Memoir of the Writer's Life,* 115–48. New York: Ballantine, 2005.

Lovgren, Stefan. "Animal Myths Busted." *National Geographic Kids* (blog), n.d. https://kids.nationalgeographic.com/nature/article/animal-myths-busted.

Mani. "Fieldfares Poop on Their Enemies." *Similar But Different in the Animal Kingdom* (blog), September 1, 2022. https://similarbutdifferentanimals.com/2022/09/01/fieldfares-poop-on-their-enemies/.

Martelle, Amélie. "Picasso and the Art of Children: Let Textiles Talk Log #7." *Stedelijk Studies* (blog), February 18, 2022. https://stedelijkstudies.com/picasso-and-the-art-of-children/.

McCollam, Dan. *All about Releasing Creativity.* YouVersion Bible App. https://www.bible.com/reading-plans/15271-all-about-releasing-creativity/day/1.

McEvoy, Ben. "26 Ways to Defeat Writer's Block (Advice from 10 Great Authors)." *Benjamin McEvoy* (blog), Feburary 12, 2020. https://benjaminmcevoy.com/26-ways-to-defeat-writers-block-advice-from-10-great-authors/.

Mckenna, Phil. "Butterflies Remember Caterpillar Experiences." *New Scientist,* March 5, 2008. https://www.newscientist.com/article/dn13412-butterflies-remember-caterpillar-experiences/.

McKittrick, Joanna. "How Do Woodpeckers Avoid Brain Injury?" *The Conversation* (blog), January 31, 2020. https://theconversation.com/how-do-woodpeckers-avoid-brain-injury-120489.

Myers, Scott. "Almost All Good Writing Begins with Terrible First Efforts." *Go into the Story* (blog), November 1, 2013. https://gointothestory.blcklst.com/almost-all-good-writing-begins-with-terrible-first-efforts-1312662100c9.

National Oceanic and Atmospheric Administration. "How Many Species Live in the Ocean?" https://oceanservice.noaa.gov/facts/ocean-species.html.

"9 Brains, 3 Hearts: Some Wild Facts about Octopuses." *Associated Press,* January 22, 2019. https://apnews.com/article/ba6e3fa5bb804565b9d6d666b6d40a73.

O'Connor, Flannery. "Catholic Novelists and Their Readers." In *Mystery and Manners: Occasional Prose,* edited by Sally Fitzgerald and Robert Fitzgerald, 169–90. New York: Farrar, Straus & Giroux, 1970.

———. "The Church and the Fiction Writer." In *Mystery and Manners: Occasional Prose,* edited by Sally Fitzgerald and Robert Fitzgerald, 143–53. New York: Farrar, Straus & Giroux, 1970.

———. *The Complete Stories of Flannery O'Connor.* New York: Farrar, Straus & Giroux,

———. "The Fiction Writer and His Country." In *Mystery and Manners: Occasional Prose*, edited by Sally Fitzgerald and Robert Fitzgerald, 25–35. New York: Farrar, Straus & Giroux, 1970.

———. *The Habit of Being: Letters of Flannery O'Connor*. Edited by Sally Fitzgerald. New York: Vintage, 1980.

———. "Novelist and Believer." In *Mystery and Manners: Occasional Prose*, edited by Sally Fitzgerald and Robert Fitzgerald, 154–68. New York: Farrar, Straus & Giroux, 1970.

———. "Some Aspects of the Grotesque in Southern Fiction." In *Mystery and Manners: Occasional Prose*, edited by Sally Fitzgerald and Robert Fitzgerald, 36–50. New York: Farrar, Straus & Giroux, 1970.

Onwujiarri, Tony. "18 Amazing Facts on Earth's Perfect Location in Space." *GulpMatrix* (blog), February 26, 2021. https://gulpmatrix.com/18-amazing-facts-on-earths-perfect-location-in-space/#gsc.tab=0.

Osterloff, Emily. "Immortal Jellyfish: The Secret to Cheating Death." *What on Earth?* (blog), n.d. https://www.nhm.ac.uk/discover/immortal-jellyfish-secret-to-cheating-death.html.

Patel, Sahil. "Five Incredible Benefits of Creativity Which Inspires[sic] You to Live a Great Life." *Medium* (blog), August 23, 2021. https://medium.com/creative-enlightenment/5-incredible-benefits-of-creativity-which-inspires-you-to-live-a-great-life-doced16f89bb.

Patenaude, Adrian. "On Becoming Creative: Creativity as Devotional Practice." *Alabaster* (blog), n.d. https://www.alabasterco.com/blogs/articles/creativity-as-devotional-practice.

Phillipsen, Ivan. "Woodpeckers." *The Science of Birds* (blog), October 29, 2020. https://www.scienceofbirds.com/blog/woodpeckers-picidae.

Raynor, Jordan. "New Series: Bezalel and the Creative Spirit of God." *Jordan Raynor* (blog), May 4, 2020. https://www.jordanraynor.com/blog/new-series-bezalel-and-the-creative-spirit-of-god.

"Rembrandt Harmensz Van Rijn: Dutch Painter of the Soul." *Christianity Today*, n.d. https://www.christianitytoday.com/history/people/musiciansartistsandwriters/rembrandt-harmensz-van-rijn.html.

Riney, J. "How Much Wood Can a Woodpecker Peck? The Science Behind a Woodpecker's Anatomy." *Biomechanics in the Wild* (blog), September 30, 2019. https://sites.nd.edu/biomechanics-in-the-wild/2019/09/30/how-much-wood-can-a-woodpecker-peck-the-science-behind-a-woodpeckers-anatomy/.

Rodriguez, Tori. "Creativity Predicts a Longer Life: The Trait of Openness Improves Health Through Creativity." *Scientific American*, September 1, 2012. https://www.scientificamerican.com/article/open-mind-longer-life/

Scafe, Shawna. "Christian Women and the Gift of Creativity (#createifcreated)." *A Little Light* (blog), n.d. https://alittlelight.ca/find-your-purpose/createifcreated/.

Scott, S. J. "23 Good Work Habit Examples to Build a Successful Career." *Develop Good Habits* (blog), September 30, 2022. https://www.developgoodhabits.com/good-workplace-habits/.

Sedgwick, Icy. "7 Ways to Refill Your Creative Well." *Confident Life* (blog), n.d. https://www.confidentlife.com.au/7-ways-refill-creative-well/.

Shaffer, Evie. "The Creative's Role in God's Invisible Kingdom." *Alabaster* (blog), n.d. https://www.alabasterco.com/blogs/articles/creatives-role-in-gods-invisible-kingdom.

BIBLIOGRAPHY

Shapka, Lindsay. "A Dose of Inspiration: Quotes by Writers, Actors, and More to Inspire Travel and Adventure." *The Anthrotorian*, October 13, 2014. https://theanthrotorian.com/culture/2014/10/13/14x0wz8sgircokh6ek9r0q2xgqnsac.

Siegel, Ethan. "Earth Is Drifting Away from the Sun, and So Are All the Planets." *Forbes*, January 3, 2019. https://www.forbes.com/sites/startswithabang/2019/01/03/earth-is-drifting-away-from-the-sun-and-so-are-all-the-planets/?sh=2c6900586f7d.

"Simple Tips for Living a Creative Life." *Creatives Doing Business* (blog), September 24, 2022. https://www.creativesdoingbusiness.com/blog/tips-for-living-creative-life.

"16 Powerful Benefits of Writing by Hand." *Vanilla Papers*, July 29, 2019. https://vanillapapers.net/2019/07/29/9-powerful-benefits-writing-by-hand/.

Skillicorn, Nick. "What Is Creativity? The Definition, History, and Science of Creativity." *Idea to Value*, May 2021. https://www.ideatovalue.com/crea/nickskillicorn/2021/05/what-is-creativity-the-definition-history-and-science-of-creativity/.

Spencer, Joanne. "Duck-Billed Platypus." https://animalcorner.org/animals/duck-billed-platypus/.

Sugarek, Trish. "An Interview with Tasha Alexander, Part 3." *Writer at Play* (blog), September 19, 2013. https://www.writeratplay.com/2013/09/19/an-interview-with-tasha-alexander-part-3-link/.

TeachThought Staff. "The Significant Benefits of Creativity in the Classroom." *TeachThought* (blog), November 15, 2019. https://www.teachthought.com/learning/benefits-creativity/.

Terry, Thomas J., and J. Ryan Lister. *Images and Idols: Creativity for the Christian Life*. Chicago: Moody, 2018.

"30 Surprising Facts about How We Spend Our Time." *Microsoft Start* (blog), December 5, 2018. https://www.msn.com/en-nz/lifestyle/lifestyle-slideshows/30-surprising-facts-about-how-we-spend-our-time/ss-BBjdTQc.

Thompson, Derek. "Your Day in a Chart: 10 Cool Facts about How Americans Spend Our [sic] Time." *The Atlantic*, June 25, 2012. https://www.theatlantic.com/business/archive/2012/06/your-day-in-a-chart-10-cool-facts-about-how-americans-spend-our-time/258967/.

Thoreau, Henry David. *Walden*. New York: Dover, 1995.

———. "Walking." In *The Portable Thoreau*, edited by Jeffrey S. Cramer, 555–89. New York: Penguin, 2012.

Thorp, Clare. "How Boredom Can Spark Creativity." *BBC*, May 22, 2020. https://www.bbc.com/culture/article/20200522-how-boredom-can-spark-creativity.

Times Educational Supplement. "Growth Mindset Quotes from the Stars Décor." https://www.tes.com/en-us/teaching-resource/growth-mindset-quotes-from-the-stars-decor-11362086.

Tommey, Matt. *Unlocking the Heart of the Artist*. YouVersion Bible App. https://www.bible.com/en/reading-plans/14601.

"20 Reasons to Write by Hand, According to Science." Top Education Degrees. https://www.topeducationdegrees.org/proven-reasons-to-write-by-hand/.

United Nations Educational, Scientific and Cultural Organization. "Ocean Life: The Marine Age of Discovery." https://www.unesco.org/en/articles/ocean-life-marine-age-discovery.

USAHavana. "The Privileged Planet." *YouTube*, July 21, 2014. https://www.youtube.com/watch?v=QmIc42oRjm8.

Van Gogh Museum. "Letter to Theo van Gogh, January 1874, Letter #17." VanGogh Museum, https://vangoghletters.org/vg/letters/let017/letter.html.

Van Gogh, Vincent. "Letter 09/09/1882." https://www.vincentvangogh.org/letter-1882-09-09.jsp.

VanHelder, Mike. "Scientists Finally Have Evidence That Frigatebirds Sleep While Flying." *Audubon*, August 11, 2016. https://www.audubon.org/news/scientists-finally-have-evidence-frigatebirds-sleep-while-flying.

Wardle, Duncan. "So, You Think You're Not Creative?" *Ascend*, March 29, 2021. https://hbr.org/2021/03/so-you-think-youre-not-creative.

Warne, Kennedy. "The Amazing Albatrosses." *Smithsonian Magazine*, September 2007. https://www.smithsonianmag.com/science-nature/the-amazing-albatrosses-162515529/.

Warren, Colleen. *Annie Dillard and the Word Made Flesh: An Incarnational Theory of Language*. Lehigh, PA: Lehigh University Press, 2010.

Webb, Paul. "Overview of the Oceans." In *Introduction to Oceanography*. https://rwu.pressbooks.pub/webboceanography/chapter/1-1-overview-of-the-oceans/.

Wendel, JoAnna. "How Fast Does the Earth Move?" *Live Science* (blog), June 27, 2021. https://www.livescience.com/how-fast-does-earth-move.html.

"Why Do All Bamboo Trees Flower at Once Irrespective of When They Are Planted?" https://www.quora.com/Why-do-all-bamboo-trees-flower-at-once-irrespective-of-when-they-are-planted.

Yancey, Philip, and Paul Brand. "Breath." In *In the Likeness of God*, 397–410. Grand Rapids, MI: Zondervan, 2004.

Youngling, R. J. "You Can't Edit a Blank Page." *Youngling Research* (blog), May 29, 2019. https://www.younglingresearch.com/essays/edit.

Ziglar, Zig. "Mistakes Are Proof That You Are Trying." *Twitter*, October 15, 2021. https://twitter.com/TheZigZiglar/status/1448868742172139522.

www.ingramcontent.com/pod-product-compliance
Lightning Source LLC
Chambersburg PA
CBHW031503160426
43195CB00010BB/1085